THIS JOURNAL
BELONGS TO:

....

....

....

STERLING
New York

An Imprint of Sterling Publishing Co., Inc.
1166 Avenue of the Americas
New York, NY 10036

ISBN: 978-1-4549-3739-5

ted in Canada by Sterling Publishing Co., Inc.
anadian Manda Group, 664 Annette Street
Toronto, Ontario M6S 2C8, Canada
he United Kingdom by GMC Distribution Services
High Street, Lewes, East Sussex BN7 1XU, England
ibuted in Australia by NewSouth Books
New South Wales, Sydney, NSW 2052, Australia

about custom editions, special sales, and premium
urchases, please contact Sterling Special Sales at
89 or specialsales@sterlingpublishing.com.

Manufactured in China

2 4 6 8 10 9 75 3 1

sterlingpublishing.com

Interior design by Scott Russo
design by Elizabeth Mihaltse Lindy

icture Credits: Depositphotos

RESI
JO

5 MIN
ST

Cover

INTRODUCTION

Life has a way of throwing us curveballs. The promotion you wanted may be given to someone else. That rock-solid relationship you thought would last forever may stall out or disappear unexpectedly. A family member or friend may pass away. A critical illness could appear just as you've made positive changes for your health. Or you may experience a financial hardship you never thought could happen to you.

Whatever challenges and hardships you may face, it is important to develop skills to help you overcome adversity and become a more resilient person who can get through difficulties and bounce back. Every human being has the capacity to be resilient. It is part of who we all are; it's built into our DNA to survive. However, at times we find ourselves reaching for tools, reassurances, inspirations, or connections to help us traverse the most difficult moments.

Incorporating the latest psychology and neuroscience research, this journal will provide you with science-based tools—as well as inspirational quotes, stories, and writing prompts—to strengthen your resilience. It will help you establish new behaviors, embrace positive thoughts, and be proactive. It will bring you closer to developing habits that will assist you in navigating life challenges and become stronger from them. Dare I say the work in this journal will help you become more "bounce back-able."

As you journal, you might feel like you're doing the same types of exercises over and over. That's by design: ten specific resilience traits are woven throughout these pages. You will also notice that there are some themes subtly rotating within four-week cycles. These have been strategically planned out to reinforce key areas of growth as follows: setting priorities (prioritizing happiness and/or making commitments to yourself); offering kindness to others, both anonymously or openly, as well as being kind to yourself; exploring the concepts of acceptance and the power of forgiveness; and establishing a practice of deliberately expressing gratitude, appreciating others, and regularly acknowledging yourself.

We're trying to create new, healthier habits—ones shown to boost resilience—through repetition. And who knows? As you get to later entries, you might even have a fresher take on an earlier prompt.

Allow these five-minute journaling prompts to be the start of your journey toward a happier future. This time is just for you. Enjoy it!

Want to Learn How to Bounce Back Faster? We all possess resilience; most of us can get over the little things pretty easily. But what we're talking about now is how to bounce back from the bigger disappointments: the challenges of life, work, relationships, and health—basically, the pieces of life that don't necessarily make you happy. The good news, according to the American Psychological Association, is that resilience isn't something you either possess or do not have. Rather, it's a habit that's reinforced and strengthened by behaviors, thoughts, and actions. It just takes practice.

Today Write about your decision to hone your resilience skill set. Why is this important to you? What would the ultimate outcome be if you were able to integrate new strategies to help you in challenging times? How would it lead to a happier life?

_____

_____

_____

_____

_____

_____

_____

Remembering the Past You've triumphed before. You've bounced back and kept on going. Remembering that you've moved beyond perceived challenges is an important part of reinforcing that you can do it again and again when needed. Studies by metaphysician Raymond Holliwell show that like attracts like. However, you must train your brain to focus on the positive aspects of any situation. Focusing on the positive aspects reminds your brain that it's possible to resolve the issue, and it will therefore seek out the positive solution to create that end goal. More on this on Week 1/Day 4.

Today Write about a challenge you've experienced in the past and how you overcame it. Notice how this makes you feel; does it evoke a feeling of relief, joy, or triumph?

_____

_____

_____

_____

_____

_____

_____

_____

What Makes You Happy? This is a big question to start with! What is it that makes you happy? Separate what you have been told *should* make you happy. Consider what actually makes you *smile*, warms your heart, and makes you feel alive.

Today Write about the various things that make you happy in your life right now and what other things you'd like to experience. This is purely subjective. There are no right or wrong answers here, only what truly resides inside of you. We will make this exercise a frequent one throughout the journal.

_____

_____

_____

_____

_____

_____

_____

_____

_____

_____

Date_____

Setting Your Priorities There are many things that make us happy. But are they a priority in your life? Raymond Holliwell teaches that what you focus on expands into your life—it literally materializes. If you are constantly thinking about chocolate, all of a sudden you will see chocolate everywhere! Your subconscious mind seeks out the object of your desire. In order to foster resilience, the pattern or habit of focusing on what you no longer want in your life needs to be interrupted so you can see the possibilities for your future.

Today Create a simple list of three to five priorities you want to set for yourself over the next couple weeks. This is not a goal list. Consciously shift your subconscious mind by creating a list of things you want more of in your life, whether it's going to the gym or reading. Give your subconscious the right stuff to focus on and seek out rather than the negative or hard stuff.

_____

_____

_____

_____

_____

_____

_____

Start with Yourself James Clear, author of *Atomic Habits*, writes: "I believe the best way to change the world is in concentric circles: start with yourself and work your way out from there. If you get yourself sorted out, then that is one less person for the world to worry about. You'll be in a position to contribute rather than consume. You will add order rather than disorder."

Today Write about what this prompt means to you. Are you in the habit of thinking about yourself first?

_____

_____

_____

_____

_____

_____

_____

_____

_____

_____

Mind-Changing Creating sustained happiness and contentment with life requires a positive frame of mind that gratitude can provide. Dr. Emma Seppälä states in her book *The Happiness Track* that if you make gratitude and thankfulness part of your life, you're more likely to experience positive results than had you not.

Today Write about a time you felt extremely grateful. How did it affect other aspects of your life?

_____

_____

_____

_____

_____

_____

_____

_____

_____

_____

_____

It Adds Up Repetition creates and reinforces habits. Dr. Brené Brown says, "Joy, collected over time, fuels resilience—ensuring we'll have reservoirs of emotional strength when hard things do happen."

Today Make a list of five to ten things that bring you joy in your life. Put a star next to two or three you can work into your week. Build the habit of joy!

_____

_____

_____

_____

_____

_____

_____

_____

_____

_____

_____

Routine Results Northwest University researchers found that having a daily routine helps reduce stress and creates a sense of safety by removing the constant worry about when things will get done.

Today Write about a part of your daily routine that makes you feel good.

_____

_____

_____

_____

_____

_____

_____

_____

_____

_____

_____

_____

_____

_____

Rising Again Sandy lost her job while in the middle of a divorce. The prospects were frightening, to say the least. While she and I were talking about it over a cup of coffee, she vowed not to let this double whammy define the rest of her life. A quote often attributed to Carl Jung says it best: "I am not what happened to me, I am what I choose to become." Although Sandy allowed herself to fall apart and mourn for a little while, she also embraced her choice to find a new path.

Today Write about what you are now choosing to become.

_____

_____

_____

_____

_____

_____

_____

_____

_____

_____

Sandy's Becoming While it didn't happen all at once, Sandy did change careers—from human resources to graphic design—which allowed her to utilize her brilliant, creative mind. She also began to make more conscious choices about the type of person she wanted to meet as opposed to the types she'd dated before getting married, who were a bit less flexible and understanding than she'd really liked. She craved a closer connection, one filled with communication and a bit of spontaneity, to reflect her newfound self-confidence. Both were choices that validated being more assertive in choosing what she wanted her life to be like.

Today Write about the areas of your life you'd like to improve to become the person you identified in yesterday's entry.

_____

_____

_____

_____

_____

_____

_____

_____

Cancel Out the Negative Did you know that it takes five times the number of positive engagements to erase the effects of a single negative interaction? Dr. John M. Gottman, a psychologist, researcher, and author, calls this 5:1 ratio the "magic ratio" to maintaining happy relationships.

Today Consider the state of your closest relationships. Write about one that could use a few more positive interactions to help it thrive.

_____

_____

_____

_____

_____

_____

_____

_____

_____

_____

_____

_____

Ninety Seconds Harvard-trained neuroanatomist Dr. Jill Bolte Taylor concluded that when a person has a reaction to an event, a chemical process happens in the body within the first ninety seconds. Anything thereafter is an emotional response pattern or "loop" generated by the individual, who keeps thinking the same thoughts. In order to interrupt the loop, try reaching for positive processing language, such as "I can figure this out," "Let me clear away the old so I can improve this process," or "There's something better waiting for me." My personal mantra is "Everything works out for me. Let's see what's on the other side!"

Today Write a simple interruption statement you can utilize to avoid being stuck in an emotional response loop. You are not a robot, so make it personal.

_____

_____

_____

_____

_____

_____

_____

Mood Balancing Serotonin is a mood stabilizer. When we do good for someone else, we experience a release of serotonin that makes us feel good, too. Acts of kindness can be small or large. They may be disguised as doing something special for someone during the course of your normal everyday activities or by offering a stranger a helping hand or a kind word.

Today Have you made a simple gesture of kindness to someone recently? Write about how it felt.

_____

_____

_____

_____

_____

_____

_____

_____

_____

_____

Random Acts of Kindness Psychologist Sonja Lyubomirsky found that intentionally demonstrating acts of kindness helps the giver have a more positive self-image and feel happier. In her study, those who committed to performing five or six random acts of kindness per week felt happier than those who did not. Dr. Lyubomirsky also found that when all six were done in the span of one day, the effect was even greater.

Today Think back over the last week. Jot down five or six random acts of kindness you performed, or identify moments where you could act kindly in the future.

_____

_____

_____

_____

_____

_____

_____

_____

_____

_____

Date_____   **Week 3 • Day 1**

Bounce Back Tip Courage isn't necessarily about being heroic. Courage is the act of doing something even if it scares you.

Today Write about something you know you need to do but haven't done yet. Identify the fear that is preventing you from taking action.

_____

_____

_____

_____

_____

_____

_____

_____

_____

_____

_____

_____

_____

One Size Doesn't Fit All We typically explain resilience as *emotional* resilience in its most general form. Psychotherapist Joshua Miles explains that the term *emotional resilience* refers to how we manage stress, trauma, or other emotionally charged events in our lives. Over the next few days, we'll explore more specific types of resilience that we can foster.

Today Write about a part of your emotional resilience that you'd like to improve.

_____

_____

_____

_____

_____

_____

_____

_____

_____

_____

_____

_____

_____

Natural Protection *Inherent* resilience, Joshua Miles says, is the catalyst that propels children to explore the world around them, through play and risk-taking. It is how they learn what is safe.

Today Write about a time from your childhood when you tested the world around you. What is that memory, and what did it teach you?

_____

_____

_____

_____

_____

_____

_____

_____

_____

_____

In the Moment *Adaptive* resilience, Miles says, "occurs at different points in our lives, and is usually brought about through a difficult or challenging experience. . . . [Adaptive resilience] needs to be learnt on the spot and can give us the ability to manage stresses and pain."

Consider these as moments where you can strengthen your adaptability.

Today Write about a time you had that moment when you realized you successfully adapted during a challenging time.

_____

_____

_____

_____

_____

_____

_____

_____

_____

_____

_____

Using Your Memory Muscle Another type of resilience Miles discusses is *learned* resilience. This resilience is built when we learn from and draw on the experiences of the past during stressful times. We build mechanisms for managing the challenge and then find ways to draw on previously unknown inner strength.

Today Write about a previously unknown strength you've had to draw upon to carry you through a big challenge.

_____

_____

_____

_____

_____

_____

_____

_____

_____

_____

_____

To Be Human If you're living, breathing, and engaging in life, you will make mistakes. You also risk being hurt. But you also have the opportunity to grow, change, adapt, explore, and be open to a bigger life than you may currently be experiencing at this moment.

Today Write about what this means to you. Are the risks worth the rewards?

_____

_____

_____

_____

_____

_____

_____

_____

_____

_____

_____

Let It Go Researchers at the Mayo Clinic found that when you let go of a grudge, you no longer feel the need to define your life by how you were hurt. Oftentimes after releasing their grudges, people found more empathy and compassion for those they felt caused an offense.

Today Write about a grudge you let go of many years ago and how your perception of that person may be different now.

_____

_____

_____

_____

_____

_____

_____

_____

_____

_____

_____

Storytelling We sometimes form unhealthy attachments to the stories we tell ourselves. Lorna Phillips, a lawyer and a leadership and governance strategist, explains: "If a bad thing happened to us in the past, we tend to identify with it, defining it as 'us,' and then we spend our time and energy trying to prevent it from ever happening again." While the story is in our past, we can easily engage in the fear of that experience at any moment in our present. Phillips reminds us that we are not the experience. "You only become frightened when you engross yourself in your memory of the past and, using your imagination to re-create your memories, you put them into a future that hasn't yet arrived."

Today Write about a story you keep telling yourself that creates fear about your future.

_____

_____

_____

_____

_____

_____

_____

Drama Drain Drama is an energy-sucking exchange; it zaps your emotional resilience. Stress expert, author, and founder of nonprofit HeartMath Doc Childre, and HeartMath president and CEO Deborah Rozman say: "When we're low on resilience, we tend to add extra drama to a problem, which magnifies the situation and creates even more drain. And that's when we spin out of control, make mistakes, say things we later regret, ignore our health, and so on."

Today Make a list of current situations that may be playing out in your daily life with too much drama—big or small. The drama can be internally or externally created.

_____

_____

_____

_____

_____

_____

_____

_____

_____

Clocking Your Time Drama also takes up a lot of time in your life. If you break it down into smaller chunks, you will see that it is a multifaceted time waster, from time spent figuring out solutions to rethinking and overthinking the situation.

Today Look at yesterday's list of dramatic situations. Pick one and calculate how much time it's taken up. What would you have preferred to do with that time?

_____

_____

_____

_____

_____

_____

_____

_____

_____

_____

_____

Slowing Down Stress Neuroscientist and author Daniel J. Levitin found that patients who listened to music experienced less anxiety and lower cortisol levels than those who hadn't.

Today Build a playlist of new music you'd like to listen to regularly to help you destress, or identify a live music event you'd like to attend.

_____

_____

_____

_____

_____

_____

_____

_____

_____

_____

_____

_____

Focusing Each person has the ability to find gratefulness, thanks, and appreciation in their lives. By doing so, you focus more on what is positive, rather than negative, in your life. Welcome to our monthly practice of gratitude. (Of course, you are welcome to jot down what you're grateful for on *any* day.)

Today Write about three things that you feel grateful for in your life.

_____

_____

_____

_____

_____

_____

_____

_____

_____

_____

_____

Making Today Count Starting the day with an expectation of good things happening in your life is a habit worth developing.

Today Write about what you're looking forward to today or tomorrow.

_____

_____

_____

_____

_____

_____

_____

_____

_____

_____

_____

_____

_____

_____

365 Days In his best-selling book *A Simple Act of Gratitude*, John Kralik charts the amazing life-transforming shifts he experienced by handwriting a thank-you note every day.

Today Make a quick list of ten or so people to whom you could send a thank-you note. Handwrite the notes and mail them.

➤ This exercise will count toward your gratitude practice in a few days.

_____

_____

_____

_____

_____

_____

_____

_____

_____

_____

_____

_____

Laughter as Medicine In her book *Habits of a Happy Brain*, Dr. Loretta Graziano Breuning notes that laughter is a natural stress reliever because it releases endorphins. Look back in your memory for a time when you laughed so hard you almost cried. Now make a mental imprint of this episode, to be used during times when you're experiencing stress.

Today Write about that experience. Are you smiling already?

_____

_____

_____

_____

_____

_____

_____

_____

_____

_____

_____

Finding Your Way One of Rumi's most famous quotes is "What you seek is seeking you." It may sound hokey, but what you are seeking is closer than you think. It's about opening your mind up to the possibility.

Today Write about a desire of your heart, and end with three sentences on why it is possible. Don't worry about how it'll happen. Just focus on the desire.

_____

_____

_____

_____

_____

_____

_____

_____

_____

_____

_____

Making Room Psychology professor Samantha Heintzelman says that living an ordered life—especially one that includes daily routines—also lays the groundwork for the pursuit of larger goals that lead to purpose and significance.

Today Write about what order means to you in your life.

_____

_____

_____

_____

_____

_____

_____

_____

_____

_____

_____

_____

Dreams There are times when a dream dies—when our whole experience of chasing or achieving that dream ends. Acknowledging the pain and allowing ourselves to grieve that loss is a step toward recovery.

Today Write about a dream that you've had to let go of. Do you remember grieving?

_____

_____

_____

_____

_____

_____

_____

_____

_____

_____

_____

_____

_____

Twenty Seconds Emily and Amelia Nagoski, coauthors of *Burnout: The Secret to Solving the Stress Cycle*, recommend hugging someone you love for twenty seconds a day in order to reduce stress. Hugging lowers blood pressure and stimulates the release of oxytocin, a hormone that can shift you out of being stressed and into a calmer state.

Today Write about how the last really good hug you received made you feel.

➤ **Make a point of getting one of those hugs today.**

_____

_____

_____

_____

_____

_____

_____

_____

_____

_____

Journal Your Way to Health A 2003 study by Drs. Michael McCullough and Robert A. Emmons published in the *Journal of Personality and Social Psychology* found that people who kept a gratitude journal reported increased well-being overall. They exercised more (approximately 40 minutes per week), felt that life was better (approximately 8 percent better), and had increased optimism (approximately 5 percent more).

Today Write about how the gratitude exercises over the last few weeks have helped your feeling of well-being.

_____

_____

_____

_____

_____

_____

_____

_____

_____

_____

Burnout Relief Author and startup advisor Sarah Kathleen Peck suggests designating one or two days a week to sleep in. Alternately, add a nap on the weekends. Studies have shown that those who are sleep-deprived react negatively to stressors.

Today Start by scheduling a nap into your week. Write down the day and time when you will do this.

_____

_____

_____

_____

_____

_____

_____

_____

_____

_____

_____

_____

Powerful People According to Liz Ryan, author of the *Reinvention Roadmap*, one of the most important life lessons you can learn by failing is knowing that even when you feel your lowest, no one can take away your resilience, ethics, and the other qualities that make you a powerful, wonderful you.

Today Make a list of the amazing qualities that make you uniquely *you*.

_____

_____

_____

_____

_____

_____

_____

_____

_____

_____

Building Your Muscles Getting back up or bouncing back when you are feeling down creates a positive habit, Ryan explains. Doing so becomes a muscle memory that, in essence, tells your mind, "Of course we're getting back up, we've done this many times before."

Today Write about what this habit means to you.

_____

_____

_____

_____

_____

_____

_____

_____

_____

_____

_____

_____

_____

Pioneering a Break Dr. Kristin Neff, an associate psychology professor, created a Self-Compassion Break system to help deal with feelings of overwhelm and stress. The first step in this process is to become mindful, without judgment or self-analyzing. Say one of these phrases: "This is a moment of suffering" or "This hurts" or "This is stress." Place your hands over your heart, and speak your identifying statement. Pause for a moment.

Today Write about how this experience might feel.

_____

_____

_____

_____

_____

_____

_____

_____

_____

_____

Breaking Down Isolation You are not alone. We are never alone. Whatever the circumstance may be, someone, some-where has experienced the same deeply painful emotions you have. The next step in Neff's process is to pick one of the following phrases to say to yourself: "Suffering is part of life" or "We all feel this way some days" or "We all struggle in our lives at times." Take a deep breath.

Today Ask yourself which of these statements resonates with you most. Write about your beliefs around that statement.

_____

_____

_____

_____

_____

_____

_____

_____

_____

Offer Yourself Kindness The last step in the Self-Compassion Break system is to place your hands on your heart and say, "May I give myself compassion" or "May I accept myself as I am" or "May I be patient."

Today Write about the kindness statement that resonates best with you and why.

_____

_____

_____

_____

_____

_____

_____

_____

_____

_____

_____

_____

Just Breathe Place all three statements you've selected from Neff's system into one list. The next time you feel overwhelmed, stressed out, or anxious, try utilizing the statements in a mindfulness exercise: Place your hands over your heart and slowly recite the statements. Try it now. Keep breathing. Allow the words to go deep into your being, becoming a deliberate act of self-kindness.

Today Write about how this mindfulness tool affected you. Did you become emotional, peaceful, or something else?

_____

_____

_____

_____

_____

_____

_____

_____

_____

_____

Feeling Good by Doing Good Medical intuitive and best-selling author Carolyn Myss wrote an entire book, *Invisible Acts of Power*, on the healing power that comes from human kindnesses. Myss says that kind, generous, or compassionate actions—what she calls invisible acts of power—create a state of grace for both the giver and the receiver. Compassion is one part of the equation she shares. When we have compassion for others, we are also able to have compassion and kindness for ourselves. We will establish a regular ritual of performing intentional acts of kindness practice.

Today Consider three random acts of kindness you could do in the next few days that will nurture, uplift, or support someone. It could be for someone you know, or it could be for yourself. Having compassion for yourself is just as healing as having it for others.

_____

_____

_____

_____

_____

_____

_____

Social Connections Dr. Loretta Graziano Breuning's work contends that serotonin is stimulated by social importance, or the connection to others you admire and respect when you are engaged with them positively. One example would be to enjoy even the smallest amount of healthy influence you've had on another person.

Today Reach out to someone you know and ask them how you have influenced or improved their life. Write out those details. How did it feel to hear this?

_____

_____

_____

_____

_____

_____

_____

_____

_____

_____

_____

Exploration Sheryl Sandberg, COO of Facebook and best-selling author of *Lean In*, gave the commencement address at the University of California, Berkeley in 2016. She inspired the graduates with her speech on resilience: "You are not born with a fixed amount of resilience. Like a muscle, you can build it up, draw on it when you need it. In that process, you will figure out who you really are, and you just might become the very best version of yourself."

Today Write about a part of yourself that has been strengthened recently.

_____

_____

_____

_____

_____

_____

_____

_____

_____

Emotional Resilience Trait #1 The experts at HeartMath have outlined ten traits demonstrated by emotionally resilient people. We will be introducing these traits at intervals throughout this journal. The first trait to note is that resilient people make self-care a priority.

Today Write about the self-care practice you currently have. Is it enough? If not, what can you do for yourself this week that will make you feel cared for and nourished?

_____

_____

_____

_____

_____

_____

_____

_____

_____

_____

_____

Minimizing Drama Create more peace and space in your life by reducing drama. Even when dealing with a critical issue, drama can take on a life of its own. Oftentimes an outside observer can objectively help you sort out what is necessary to focus your energy on and what's not worth your time. Consider this a simple decluttering exercise: Think about the things that zap your energy emotionally, mentally, and physically, and decide which ones you can eliminate.

Today Identify the friend or professional who can help you sort through your current issue. On the first line below, write the issue or drama you want to work on. Next, write the name of the person who will help you and a deadline for when you will reach out to ask for help.

➤ **Send a text or e-mail to that person while this is at the top of your mind—meaning *right now*.**

_____

_____

_____

_____

_____

_____

_____

No-Drama Zone As my husband went through cancer treatment for a total of seven years, we learned to limit the drama in our lives. There was too much on our plates to let unnecessary distractions take us away from managing his treatment and our lives. We declared our home a drama-free zone. If guests created drama, they weren't invited back; it was one of the ways we were able to preserve our sanity.

Today Consider how you can create your own drama-free zone. Write out the boundaries you could set up to facilitate that safe space in your life.

_____

_____

_____

_____

_____

_____

_____

_____

_____

Rain Creates Small Streams Over a period of time, streams become rivers. Habits and patterns work similarly. Experiences cause neurons to fire in your brain. In time, after a lot of firing, they become hardwired into your brain to create a "river," or default coping mechanism. It's why some habits are so hard to break.

Today Write about one or two patterns you'd like to change.

_____

_____

_____

_____

_____

_____

_____

_____

_____

_____

_____

A New Mantra The act of fully embracing self-acceptance is illustrated by a wonderful French saying: *Tout comprendre c'est tout pardonner.* Translated, it means "to understand all is to forgive all." In understanding there is the possibility to have compassion for yourself and for others.

Today Write about an opportunity you may have to understand and to "forgive all."

_____

_____

_____

_____

_____

_____

_____

_____

_____

_____

_____

Numerous Choices There are literally thousands of healing modalities in the world. Former clinical social worker and psychotherapist Kelly Sullivan Ruta says, "The way out is to connect within." To be able to hear your inner voice is key to overcoming whatever challenges you may face.

Today Write an honest assessment of what your inner voice sounds like.

_____

_____

_____

_____

_____

_____

_____

_____

_____

_____

_____

Knowing the Difference Ruta makes the distinction between your ego and your inner voice. Your ego is the inner critic that says you can't do something well, cuts you down, or tells you you're wrong. If you're hearing those words, it's not your inner voice. Your inner voice always calls you forward to expand. It propels you toward creativity and honesty and speaks the truth of who you are.

Today Write about what your true inner voice says when you are quiet and still.

➤ **Tune out negative voices so that you can listen to the positive truth about yourself.**

_____

_____

_____

_____

_____

_____

_____

_____

_____

Maximizing the 40 Percent According to Sonja Lyubomirsky's research, the origins of happiness are derived as follows: 50 percent from genetics, 10 percent from environmental or life circumstances, and 40 percent from ourselves. That 40 percent is under your control. That's the great news!

Today Write about the 40 percent that's under your control. What gives you joy, makes your heart sing, and opens your curious mind?

➤ Keep these things in mind while we get ready for some gratitude in a couple of days.

_____

_____

_____

_____

_____

_____

_____

_____

_____

Uncover Conditional Happiness Life circumstances and one's environment make up only 10 percent of what creates happiness. Waiting for a new job or a new relationship to make you happy means you're relying on a conditional state of happiness, which is short-lived. Doing this puts pressure on that one situation or person to make you happy.

Today Write about the conditional happiness items you may have in your patterning.

_____

_____

_____

_____

_____

_____

_____

_____

_____

_____

_____

Make Gratitude a Priority As you continue to journal through the year, you'll learn from many experts that gratitude is a magic elixir in shifting your life to a better place. Just trust the process.

Today Write about three things that you feel grateful for in your life.

_____

_____

_____

_____

_____

_____

_____

_____

_____

_____

_____

_____

_____

Revisiting Kindness One particularly tough day not too long ago, I jumped onto an overcrowded subway car and thought, *This is crazy!* As I looked around for a seat, exasperated, a woman I did not know sitting at the opposite side of the car gave me a big grin. She waved me closer and then got up and gave me her seat. I was floored by the gesture, especially because I really needed to sit down at that moment; my back was painfully out of whack. Her kindness lifted the dark cloud from over my head and made me feel seen when I needed it.

Today Write about the effect that kindness from a stranger had on you.

_____

_____

_____

_____

_____

_____

_____

_____

_____

Dose of Patience According to researchers at Northeastern University, people who are grateful for the little things in their lives exhibit more patience.

Today Consider the correlation between patience and gratitude. Where have you recently offered more patience than in the past?

_____

_____

_____

_____

_____

_____

_____

_____

_____

_____

_____

_____

_____

_____

Naturally Happy Brains Four chemicals within the human brain perpetuate happiness. Dr. Breuning identifies them as "happy brain chemicals." They are dopamine (the joy of finding what you seek), endorphins (mask pain), oxytocin (from comforting social engagement), and serotonin (from a feeling of social importance). Let's start by boosting your dopamine. Identify a small win or series of wins or accomplishments you've had in the past day or so.

Today Write about at least one of those small wins.

_____

_____

_____

_____

_____

_____

_____

_____

_____

_____

Imagining Your Day Visualization, many researchers have found, is a profound way of setting an intention or making a plan for the day. Spend a moment and ask yourself, "What do I want my day to look like?" and "What attitude would I like to embrace today? How will that play out in my day?"

Today Write about the visualization you've created for today.

_____

_____

_____

_____

_____

_____

_____

_____

_____

_____

_____

_____

_____

Date_____

Coloring with Details Visualization is far more effective, author and inner-strength coach Pamela Palladino Gold advises, when you are more specific and vivid in your description. The more color, detail, and feeling associated with the visualization, the more likely the imprint will stay with you for the entire day.

Today Write about the visualization you began yesterday, now adding a bit more detail. If this feels too overwhelming, concentrate on one aspect that feels most important to you in this moment.

_____

_____

_____

_____

_____

_____

_____

_____

_____

_____

_____

Science and Superheroes One commonality among strong leaders, according to a 2010 study at the University of Texas at Austin, is a hormone cocktail of higher testosterone and lower cortisol levels. This combination leads to more feelings of confidence. It also heightens relaxation, so handling stressful situations isn't as difficult. Who knew? Also in 2010, a team of researchers from Harvard and Columbia Universities, including psychologist and best-selling author Amy Cuddy, found that striking a confident "high-power pose" seems to create the same balance of hormones. The most well-known high-power pose is the superhero or Wonder Woman pose: standing tall with your hands on your hips, feet spread apart, shoulders straight, and chest out.

Today Take a moment to strike the superhero pose. Write about how it feels. Get beyond the silliness and stand strong. (Capes are not required!) How do you feel?

_____

_____

_____

_____

_____

_____

_____

Deploying Your Inner Hero Is it Wonder Woman, Batman, or Superman? Decide who your inner hero is and strike that pose again today. In that strong, confident hormonal cocktail is power.

Today Write about a situation where you can deploy this confidence-building tactic to create a more desirable result.

_____

_____

_____

_____

_____

_____

_____

_____

_____

_____

_____

_____

Clear Thinking The researchers at Northeastern University from Week 8/Day 7 who found that grateful people were more patient also concluded that patience contributes to more sensible decision-making.

Today Write about your level of sensible decision-making. Can it be enhanced by a bit more gratitude?

_____

_____

_____

_____

_____

_____

_____

_____

_____

_____

_____

Missing Pieces Grief recovery specialist Stephen Moeller writes that lasting emotional pain around a loss occurs due to unfinished emotional business; instead of suppressing the pain and letting it fester, try to determine "what you wish had been different, better, or more, and [address] that in a meaningful way."

Today Write about what may have gone unsaid or undone. Begin the journey of completion.

_____

_____

_____

_____

_____

_____

_____

_____

_____

_____

_____

Time for Tears Dr. Breuning encourages people to cry, but *not* to make it a habit, as crying can lower your immune system if prolonged. Crying is a necessary release of stress and tension; it stimulates endorphins to reduce the negative effects of stress.

Today Write about the last time you had a good cry. What brought it on? How did you feel afterward?

➤ **Give yourself permission to cry sometimes.**

_____

_____

_____

_____

_____

_____

_____

_____

_____

_____

_____

Hardiness Plays a Part Dr. George Bonanno, a professor of clinical psychology and a pioneer in the field of grief and resilience, suggests that hardiness is a trait that buffers extreme stress. Hardiness has three aspects. The first is to be committed to a purpose in your life. "Purpose" is very personal for each of us. A woman I know whose husband was declining into dementia became involved with training guide dogs as an outlet. As she trained each pup, she reaped their unconditional love—a comfort for her. After her husband's passing, this work took on new meaning. She took pride in knowing that her work helped make life easier for a veteran or disabled child. In her journey, she found a meaningful purpose.

Today Write about the activities, work, or issues that matter to you. Look for a common thread that could be a link to your purpose.

_____

_____

_____

_____

_____

_____

_____

Seeing the Change Dr. Bonanno notes that another aspect of hardiness is the belief that you can influence or change your environment or surroundings and the outcome of events; it is the removal of hopelessness or resignation. Begin with small steps, if needed, to influence or change your environment to lessen stress. Even seemingly insignificant actions can offer glimmers of hope.

Today Write about a time when you may have had to find that seemingly small action associated with your glimmer of hope. What and how did it change your circumstance?

_____

_____

_____

_____

_____

_____

_____

_____

_____

Lessons and Teaching Moments The third aspect of hardiness, Dr. Bonanno found, also includes the belief that you can learn from both positive and negative experiences. Life presents teaching moments in a variety of ways.

Today Write about the lessons you learned in the past that could help you through your current situation.

_____

_____

_____

_____

_____

_____

_____

_____

_____

_____

_____

_____

Exhibiting Grit *Cambridge Dictionary* defines grit as "courage and determination despite difficulty." You could also call it resolve or persistence. Grit evokes a pioneering spirit, one of going it alone and being determined to find a way.

Today Make a list of three courageous acts that demonstrated your steadfast determination and pluckiness (great word!) in your life. Next to each, briefly write about how these acts made you feel. Did you feel proud of yourself? Maybe you were amazed at your resourcefulness or dedication.

_____

_____

_____

_____

_____

_____

_____

_____

_____

_____

Date_____   **Week 10 • Day 6**

Modeling Others There are times when we can lose our hardiness or grit. Seeing these traits in others helps us to know that they are, indeed, possible to regain.

Today Write about the "grittiest" person you know. What can you learn from them?

_____

_____

_____

_____

_____

_____

_____

_____

_____

_____

_____

_____

_____

Powerful Yet Simple Author Masaru Emoto theorized that saying one simple phrase—"thank you"—to water as it froze caused the water to coalesce into beautiful, complex, and colorful crystalline patterns, while water exposed to negative statements created incomplete, dull, noncrystalline patterns. Appreciation and gratitude change your environment just as easily. Change the molecular structure of your environment by saying thank you as much as possible today.

Today List three people you have appreciation for and why.

_____

_____

_____

_____

_____

_____

_____

_____

_____

_____

Making a Choice We all have good days and bad days; days when we're cranky and annoyed (or annoying) and may not express ourselves as we wish. It's easy to have a knee-jerk reaction to something we find undesirable. But taking a couple of deep, measured breaths before reacting gives you the time and power to choose a more calm and logical response.

Today Write about a situation or personal dynamic that you wish you had reacted to differently. What would have been a more measured response?

➤ Replaying a scenario allows you to reframe the situation and practice a new solution.

_____

_____

_____

_____

_____

_____

_____

_____

Travel Bug Relationship experts Linda and Charlie Bloom suggest that you give yourself a change of scenery as a means to regain perspective, rest, restore yourself, and reconnect with the person(s) you love. This pause allows you to let go of control and break the blame cycle, and it gives you time to think about what you really want.

Today Write about a change of scenery that shifted your perceptions in the past.

➤ **These breaks can be as short as a weekend, or they can be longer. Just take one!**

_____

_____

_____

_____

_____

_____

_____

_____

_____

Emotional Resilience Trait #2 The second trait in HeartMath's list is the ability to put things into perspective. Resilient people recognize that stress and feeling overwhelmed don't define who they are. It is a moment or series of moments over a larger span of time.

Today Write about a time when stress or overwhelming circumstances overrode your self-esteem or made you doubt yourself. How did you bounce back?

_____

_____

_____

_____

_____

_____

_____

_____

_____

_____

_____

The Fight-or-Flight Response When you feel threatened or stressed, your body's adrenal glands release adrenaline and cortisol, the stress hormone, producing what is called the fight-or-flight response. If you are constantly feeling under stress without any letup, your body keeps producing cortisol. The long-term consequences of this can wreak havoc on a person's mental and physical well-being, reducing their ability to be resilient.

Today Write about a time when you experienced a high amount of stress. How did you release it?

_____

_____

_____

_____

_____

_____

_____

_____

_____

_____

The "Tend and Befriend" Response Psychologist Shelley E. Taylor found that "tend-and-befriend" is the polar opposite of fight-or-flight. When we bond with others, the brain releases what is sometimes called the cuddle hormone or love hormone: oxytocin.

Today Write about a person who, when you connect with them, helps you feel safe, taken care of, or loved. When was the last time you visited with them (including over social media, FaceTime, or Skype)?

_____

_____

_____

_____

_____

_____

_____

_____

_____

_____

Retraining Your Responses Neuroplasticity is the driver when it comes to learning. The brain learns from experiences only. Repetition causes your brain's neurons to fire and create a path of response—positively or negatively. Dr. Dan Siegel at UCLA's Mindful Awareness Research Center calls guided visualization a key tool in replacing negative experiences with positive ones. It opens the mind to play and to explore new possibilities.

Today Make a list of apps you've found that offer guided visualizations focusing on the area of your life you may want to enhance, such as positive thinking or stress reduction. Alternately, you can record your own guided meditation. Keep it short and simple.

_____

_____

_____

_____

_____

_____

_____

_____

More Than Chicken Soup Researchers have found that forgiveness promotes the production of antibodies that boost the immune system. Forgiveness also reduces levels of immune suppressants, cortisol, and adrenaline. In a study with HIV patients, those who practiced forgiveness had a higher level of immune cells.

Today Write about how you are physically feeling these days.

_____

_____

_____

_____

_____

_____

_____

_____

_____

_____

_____

_____

The What-If Card What if you could have an experience and not judge it? What if you could have a reaction and not judge that, either? Can you separate yourself from disappointing situations by simply becoming an objective observer? Try to detach self-judgmental emotions from negative experiences.

Today Consider the last challenging situation you experienced that caused you discomfort. Visualize replacing yourself with another person. Replay the situation, and observe without allowing your own personal feelings to be triggered. Write about what you see happening in the situation with all parties.

_____

_____

_____

_____

_____

_____

_____

_____

_____

An Opportunity to Reconsider the Facts Think a bit more about the exercise we did yesterday. Did you gain any further insights into your situation? Did you see anything different than what you perceived in the original situation when you imagined it happened to someone else rather than yourself?

Today Consider how your perception of the situation may have changed in the past twenty-four to thirty-six hours. Write about what you learned from an observer's point of view rather than as the participant.

_____

_____

_____

_____

_____

_____

_____

_____

_____

_____

Sleep Is More Than Just Feeling Refreshed During sleep, the immune system recharges itself and manufactures more antibodies. A study published in the peer-reviewed journal *Archives of Internal Medicine* (now called the *JAMA Internal Medicine*) showed that if you get less than seven hours of sleep every night, you're 2.94 times more likely to catch a cold. The less sleep you have, the longer the recovery time.

Today Keep track of how many hours you're sleeping over the next seven days. Just make a note at the top of each page. Naps count, too! Today, write about how you slept last night.

➤ **Before dropping off to sleep, start thinking about your gratitude list. It's coming up in a couple of days.**

_____

_____

_____

_____

_____

_____

_____

_____

_____

Sleep Solution from a Global Gypsy I've spent most of my
life traveling overseas for work. I realized pretty quickly that
it wasn't necessarily the germy airplanes that made me sick;
it was jet lag, disrupted sleep due to time zone changes, and
dehydration. It took me years to develop a protocol that would
allow me to keep my immune system strong and maintain a
clear mind while I worked. In a small, travel-size spray bottle,
I mixed lavender and wild orange essential oils with water. I'd
spray the mixture into a cloth napkin to keep with me on the
plane that I could breathe into when needed. Later, I'd lightly
spray my hotel bed linens with it. It was relaxing and comforting, and I woke up feeling very refreshed and alert.

Today Make a short list of scents that you find pleasing, calming, and relaxing. Are they floral or earthy scents? Citrus or
herbal?

_____

_____

_____

_____

_____

_____

_____

Gratitude Observations It's time! Take a moment to think back over the past few days. What are you grateful for today?

Today Write about three things you feel grateful for now.

_____

_____

_____

_____

_____

_____

_____

_____

_____

_____

_____

_____

_____

_____

Inventory of Goodness Take a moment to look around where you live. What about it makes you happy? What part makes you happiest?

Today Look around more deeply than you have in the past. Inventory even the smallest things that you appreciate about your home. Write down at least three of them.

_____

_____

_____

_____

_____

_____

_____

_____

_____

_____

_____

_____

Enjoy More, Stress Less Shifting your focus from things that stress or upset you to those you enjoy will help distract you—and that's a good thing! Focus less on the things that cause you stress and worry.

Today Write a list of three things that you can focus on enjoying today.

_____

_____

_____

_____

_____

_____

_____

_____

_____

_____

_____

_____

Happiness Is a Skill Happiness isn't something you can just find, explains Dr. Tchiki Davis, founder of the Berkeley Well-Being Institute. It's a skill you grow by learning to control, manage, and create emotional experiences that are positive.

Today Make a list of *things* that you thought would *make you happy*—such as a new job or relationship—but haven't. Awareness is key. Underneath that list, make another list of negative emotional responses you automatically lean on during stress (i.e., being argumentative, being in a state of denial, or withdrawing and not communicating). How can you better manage these reactions in order to make yourself happier?

_____

_____

_____

_____

_____

_____

_____

_____

_____

_____

Making Progress Seeing progress on projects, inside and outside of the workplace, is proven to boost morale and happiness. Researchers Teresa Amabile and Steven Kramer suggest a practice of starting your day by writing down three things you'll accomplish—*before* you open e-mails or answer phone calls. Once the three items are completed, cross them off!

Today Write a short list of the three tasks you'd like to accomplish today.

_____

_____

_____

_____

_____

_____

_____

_____

_____

_____

_____

Acknowledge Forward Movement Amabile and Kramer also encourage you to acknowledge what you have achieved. Our brains have a habit of focusing more on what may have gone wrong, no matter how small. Let's override that wiring. The trick is to do so consistently, in the same manner every day. I like to reflect on something positive during my drive home or when I'm preparing dinner.

Today Write about something you accomplished yesterday that you may not ordinarily recognize, and celebrate. Smile. You're doing great.

_____

_____

_____

_____

_____

_____

_____

_____

_____

_____

Three Choices Transformational coach Orna Walters illustrates the emotions surrounding decision-making as doors that are cold, warm, or hot. The cold door represents a choice associated with safety and familiarity. The warm door represents some risk or level of fear. And the hot door symbolizes high risk and uncertainty. People are creatures of habit; when faced with a decision, most choose the cold door—the one with the least amount of risk.

Today Consider some of the most recent decisions you've made, such as choices about your finances, relationships, health, and work life. List three to five. Next to each decision, identify those you made feeling certain and safe (cold), with some level of risk (warm), or that were highly risky (hot). Now asterisk the ones that are more typical of how you usually make decisions.

_____

_____

_____

_____

_____

_____

_____

Training Ourselves Warm doors help us learn to take more measured risks or face our fears in a gentler way. For example, if you've lost a loved one, big decisions may feel like a hot door. There is probably no need to make every financial decision for your future in that first moment. The overwhelming emotions would create enormous fear. However, transitioning to a warm-door decision might be seeking a professional's advice and putting a plan together that they could help you execute over a period of time. The goal is to teach yourself to take more risks in a measured way.

Today Write about a hot-door decision you've faced in the past. Did you take the hot door, or were you able to walk through a warm door? What happened?

_____

_____

_____

_____

_____

_____

_____

_____

Loss Template John W. James, founder of the Grief Recovery Institute, has found that most of our coping tools for grief, or for loss of any kind, are templates given to us as children. One of the most common tools is the advice that we need to be strong for others—to hold it together and not become too emotional in public. The standard response to a concerned inquiry of "How are you doing?" is typically "I'm fine," when the truth is the complete opposite—*fine* often really means **f**eelings **i**nside **n**ot **e**xpressed.

Today Write about your template for handling grief. What have you been taught is or is not appropriate?

_____

_____

_____

_____

_____

_____

_____

_____

_____

Finding Yourself Again Dr. Therese Rando's research found that when we experience loss, the first process one needs to go through is to acknowledge and understand what has passed. A secondary loss also occurs—the loss of a sense of security, of one's identity, or of traditions and routines.

Today Write about any secondary sense of loss that you may be experiencing.

_____

_____

_____

_____

_____

_____

_____

_____

_____

_____

_____

What's in a Word? *Vulnerability* is a word that holds different meanings for different people. What does it mean to you?

Today Using word association, create a list of what vulnerability means to you. Do this in rapid-fire fashion, without stopping or overthinking. At the end, review your list. What does it show you about yourself?

_____

_____

_____

_____

_____

_____

_____

_____

_____

_____

_____

_____

_____

Pain-Suppressing Endorphins Neuroscientist Dr. Billi Gordon stated that creating drama can be highly addictive. Drama causes our pituitary gland and hypothalamus to secrete endorphins, which are the pain-suppressing and pleasure-inducing chemical neurotransmitters in the brain that resemble heroin and other opiates. Without realizing it, one can become addicted to drama, even when the drama is a real-life loss of something or someone precious.

Today Write about a recent drama that may be replaying, extending, or continuing throughout the fabric of your life. Where was its source? Was it exacerbated by your reactions to specific people or events?

_____

_____

_____

_____

_____

_____

_____

_____

Asking More Questions Licensed clinical social worker and author Katie Hurley advises parents to help teach their child resilience by *not* trying to fix problems their child asks them to solve. Instead, parents should ask probing questions to help the child solve the problem on their own or talk them through creating an action plan.

Today Write three questions you could ask yourself to help resolve your current issue. It's not necessary to have the answer. The simple act of asking the right questions will get you there.

_____

_____

_____

_____

_____

_____

_____

_____

_____

_____

Fear Walking Today, consider the three doors from Week 13/ Day 4 again. Identify a current decision or series of decisions sitting in front of the hot door that feels high-risk—like a storm of fear in your life.

Today Write down a current hot fear. List what makes it so risky. Then detail a few steps toward making a decision that feels less risky and more like walking through the warm door instead of the hot one.

_____

_____

_____

_____

_____

_____

_____

_____

_____

_____

Something to Consider Orna Walters considers herself to be a pretty resilient woman. However, there are times when even she faces a hot-door decision that feels overwhelming. Her way of moving through warm and hot doors is to remind herself that she doesn't *not* do things that scare her. She chooses to do the things that will expand her life in a positive direction.

Today Write about what you are currently doing to expand your life in a positive direction.

_____

_____

_____

_____

_____

_____

_____

_____

_____

_____

_____

Identifying the Task Master Are you overly harsh with yourself? Let's find out. Consider the last situation where you were especially tough on yourself. Now, how would you have treated a friend in the same situation?

Today Create two columns below: one labeled **ME**, and the other **MY FRIEND**. Write a list of behaviors or responses for how you would have treated yourself versus how you would treat your friend.

_____

_____

_____

_____

_____

_____

_____

_____

_____

_____

_____

Sisterly Comfort Acts of kindness from other people can be cathartic. I can recall a time when I made a major mistake in my life. I was so ashamed and embarrassed, I could barely talk about it. My pride shut me down tight. In a moment when I let my guard down to my sister, she took my hand and gently said, "Ri, it's okay that you're not perfect." I cried tears of relief from these few simple words and her sweet gesture. It released so much of the pent-up judgment inside me.

Today Write about a time when someone extended a kind, compassionate gesture to you.

_____

_____

_____

_____

_____

_____

_____

_____

_____

Dopamine High Music triggers the pleasure centers in the brain that release dopamine, the happiness hormone.

Today Write the name of your favorite song, album, or playlist below. Why does this music make you so happy?

_____

_____

_____

_____

_____

_____

_____

_____

_____

_____

_____

_____

Multiple Benefits You may already know that regular self-affirmations help build a positive self-image and an optimistic mind-set. However, one of the least talked about benefits of self-affirmations is that they can make you more resilient. No matter what the challenge may be, personally or socially, a stronger sense of self helps you bounce back more quickly.

Today Write one positive affirmation for yourself. Just one.

➤ **Bonus points if you write it on a sticky note and place it on your bathroom mirror.**

_____

_____

_____

_____

_____

_____

_____

_____

_____

_____

Emotional Resilience Trait #3 Resilient individuals are compassionate people who treat others with dignity and respect, according to HeartMath.

Today Write about the level of compassion you express to others. Are you nurturing or judgmental? Do you have compassion for yourself? What do you want to work on?

_____

_____

_____

_____

_____

_____

_____

_____

_____

_____

_____

_____

The Key to Satisfaction Self-compassion is the gift of offering ourselves compassion—of receiving our own suffering with love, acceptance, and understanding. Studies have shown that those who offer themselves compassion experience a reduction in depression, stress, and anxiety, thus increasing feelings of satisfaction.

Today Write about your level of willingness to accept self-compassion and self-empathy.

_____

_____

_____

_____

_____

_____

_____

_____

_____

_____

_____

_____

Sidestepping the Judge Accepting those around you who may judge your actions is no easy task. However, as author Liz Ryan points out, they don't really matter. Embracing this philosophy helps lessen their impact on you.

Today Write about a judgment that caused you pain. What would your day look like if you didn't feel that weight over you?

_____

_____

_____

_____

_____

_____

_____

_____

_____

_____

_____

_____

Mind-Body Connections The term *psychoneuroimmunology* refers to the field of medicine dealing with the connection between our thoughts and emotions, and our neural and immune systems. Author Jennifer Read Hawthorne contends that complaints, griping, or harsh judgment of others (or of ourself) weaken our physiology, leaving us exhausted. Positive, life-affirming thoughts, on the other hand, leave us feeling energized.

Today Write about what you were doing the last time you felt energized. Spare no detail!

_____

_____

_____

_____

_____

_____

_____

_____

_____

Clearing Confusion Forgiveness, as a concept for improving one's life and relationships, is taught by many cultures and denominations. While there are various *guidelines* suggested, I have found that, simply put, forgiveness is the ability to pardon or excuse someone related to a negative or painful experience.

Today Write about a pardon or excuse you need to offer either yourself or another person.

_____

_____

_____

_____

_____

_____

_____

_____

_____

_____

Sleep Deprivation Brain dampening and fog can be a result of sleep deprivation. During sleep, your brain cleanses itself of waste proteins, say researchers from the University of Rochester Medical Center and NYU Langone Health. When you don't get enough sleep, the brain's neurons move at a slower rate and reduce decision-making, reaction times, and reasoning.

Today Write an honest assessment on your current level of brain fog. Awareness is key to changing something out of alignment in your system.

➤ **Take a nap sometime today if you are experiencing these symptoms.**

_____

_____

_____

_____

_____

_____

_____

_____

_____

Make Room for Sleep Creating a peaceful space for relaxation and sleep is a widely endorsed practice. Maybe it's tidying up the bedroom, laying out clothing for the next day so you do not have to think about it, or taking a bath for 10–15 minutes to reduce stress or anxiety.

Today Write about what would help create a more relaxed, calm environment, so you can sleep better.

➤ **Try turning off your electronic devices at least an hour before going to bed; the blue light emitted by many of these devices can delay the release of sleep-inducing melatonin.**

_____

_____

_____

_____

_____

_____

_____

_____

Sugar Cookies Cookie cutters are nice—for cookies. But as far as people go, we are all different. We want others to see our point of view. It makes us comfortable when people seem to get us, even if they don't agree with us. However, relationships aren't always neatly packaged. Practicing acceptance is paramount to creating positive relationships.

Today Write about a relationship where you fundamentally disagree with someone on an issue or issues. Does this person add a different position that could inform your own perspective? Can you accept them as they are?

➤ It's possible you'll want to include this person on your gratitude list if you've learned something valuable from the relationship. That opportunity is coming up in a few days.

_____

_____

_____

_____

_____

_____

_____

_____

Finding Satisfaction Healthier, happier, and more satisfied people are those who are connected to others. They spend a lot of time with friends and family. Professor Sonja Lyubomirsky found that positive relationships nurture and support all areas of your life.

Today Write about a relationship you'd like to strengthen in the next few days.

_____

_____

_____

_____

_____

_____

_____

_____

_____

_____

Being in the Moment Mindfulness is about being in the moment and having full awareness of what is happening. Without mindfulness, we risk overlooking small, bright, shining moments of happiness or joy.

Today Write about something wonderful that you've experienced in the last twenty-four hours.

_____

_____

_____

_____

_____

_____

_____

_____

_____

_____

_____

_____

Outmaneuver Your Default Humans possess a natural negativity bias. However, you can retrain your brain. At the end of your day, take a gratitude pause to acknowledge your progress. There will be tough days when the best you can do is say, "I'm grateful I brushed my hair." That's okay! But other days you may find yourself saying, "I'm grateful for my spouse, the work I love, and the people who made me laugh at myself today."

Today Make a list of three aspects of your life for which you are grateful.

_____

_____

_____

_____

_____

_____

_____

_____

_____

_____

Small Victories Check-In Small triumphs are as equally important as grand ones. Small steps add up to bigger strides.

Today Reflect on the past few months. What are some of your
small victories? Write a list of ten. Celebrate!

_____

_____

_____

_____

_____

_____

_____

_____

_____

_____

_____

_____

_____

_____

Rise and Shine The experiences employees have in the morning before they enter their workspace can affect their mood for the entire day, conclude Dr. Nancy Rothbard at Wharton and Dr. Steffanie Wilk at Ohio State University in a 2011 study. They suggest starting your day with something positive, like trying a less stressful route to work or singing along to your favorite song. You could also try an activity that provides fresh air and/or movement, such as taking a walk outside, gardening, or doing yoga.

Today Write about how you are currently starting your day. Are you excited or grumpy? Do you want to crawl back under your covers? What single action could you take to create a more positive mood?

_____

_____

_____

_____

_____

_____

_____

_____

_____

Top Hats and Cheshire Cats In *Alice's Adventures in Wonderland*, author Lewis Carroll provides a simple yet powerful lesson to keep taking steps forward, even though you may not know where you're going:

> *"Would you tell me, please, which way I ought to go from here?"* [said Alice]
>
> *"That depends a good deal on where you want to get to,"* said the Cat.
>
> *"I don't much care where—"* said Alice.
>
> *"Then it doesn't matter which way you go,"* said the Cat.

Today Imagine that you don't have to know every step you'll need to take right now. You just have to take the next step in front of you. Write about how that might help you to stop overthinking, obsessing, or trying to control a current challenge.

_____

_____

_____

_____

_____

_____

_____

Uniqueness Factor We often forget about the aspects of who we are that make us unique. What is unique about you? What about you adds to the world around you? Is it your persistence, your kindness, your zaniness—or something else?

Today Write about something that makes you unique and that positively influences the world around you.

_____

_____

_____

_____

_____

_____

_____

_____

_____

_____

_____

_____

Evaluating Your Bendy-ness Are you truly flexible, or are you maybe a little (or a lot) rigid? Being able to bend is a key resource in building a more resilient mind-set.

Today Describe a situation where you faced change. Consider how you reacted. Did you embrace it, fear it, or run from it? Write a little about that experience and your response.

_____

_____

_____

_____

_____

_____

_____

_____

_____

_____

_____

_____

_____

Ignorance Is Not Bliss Author Kendra Cherry observes that waiting for a problem to evaporate doesn't make it go away; it just prolongs the crisis. Solutions may not always be swift or simple. However, taking action can aid in reducing anxiety around the issue.

Today Write about a situation that you are waiting to just go away. Ask yourself why you are waiting, and list some active steps you can take to resolve the issue.

_____

_____

_____

_____

_____

_____

_____

_____

_____

_____

_____

Decision Fatigue *Decision fatigue,* a term coined by social psychologist Roy F. Baumeister, is a phenomenon that makes stable, rational human beings fall into poor decision-making choices or completely withdraw from making rational decisions. Baumeister found that we have a finite amount of energy to expend on decision-making. The more choices we make on a given day, the more difficult each one becomes for the brain to process, and sooner or later we'll look for shortcuts.

Today Write about the last time you made a poor decision due to decision fatigue and then later wondered, *How in the world could I have thought that was a good idea?*

_____

_____

_____

_____

_____

_____

_____

_____

_____

It's in the Details Making decisions is a critical aspect of everyday life, but the level of detail that goes into some decisions can become overwhelming at times. Think about what goes into planning a wedding. Even happy occasions become stressful when many different choices must be made: venue, theme, colors, flowers, music, invitations, dresses . . . and the list goes on. In the end, some people just end up saying, "Okay, whatever," because the thought of making one more decision will push them over the edge.

Today Write about a decision you made recently just because it was the easiest choice.

➤ Decision fatigue can show up in any aspect of your life.

_____

_____

_____

_____

_____

_____

_____

_____

_____

Hope Is Oxygen Neuroscientists studying the effects of hope on the brain have found that having hope causes the brain to release neurochemicals—endorphins and enkephalins—that mimic morphine. These chemicals can block both physical and emotional pain, allowing for an acceleration in healing.

Today Write about a past experience where hope propelled you forward.

_____

_____

_____

_____

_____

_____

_____

_____

_____

_____

_____

Storytelling The correlation between hope and recovery has been scientifically proven. Learning skills specialist Terry Small believes that the art of telling or hearing stories of hope can produce the same morphine-like reaction as discussed in yesterday's prompt. He considers stories to be the number one brain-state changer in existence.

Today Write about a story, movie, or YouTube clip that embodies hopefulness and how it impacts your emotional state.

_____

_____

_____

_____

_____

_____

_____

_____

_____

_____

_____

We All Experience Crises You're in it with some of the best people. When a friend, Brenda, experienced a harsh financial crisis in her life, she felt ashamed and embarrassed. She wondered how it could have happened, being that she is a high-functioning professional. She remembered a distant friend who had her finances crash and burn several years prior. Brenda always admired the way her friend dealt with the situation. Even though her friend knew it wasn't always easy, she made it to the other side.

Today Write about someone you know and admire who experienced a crisis. What part of their journey gives you hope and inspiration?

_____

_____

_____

_____

_____

_____

_____

_____

Role Models Bouncing back can sometimes be an act of courage. Susan Cain, author of *Quiet: The Power of Introverts in a World That Can't Stop Talking*, suggests finding a "quietly courageous" role model who embodies courage as a constant reminder that *yes*, you can *too*. That role model can help you stretch beyond your current limitations.

Today Write about someone you consider a quietly courageous role model, from your own life or from history.

_____

_____

_____

_____

_____

_____

_____

_____

_____

_____

Bending but Not Breaking Kendra Cherry considers flexibility an essential part of resilience. By becoming a more adaptable person, you'll be able to respond to any life crisis more easily.

Today Consider your level of flexibility. Rank yourself on a scale of 1 to 10, with 1 being inflexible and 10 being extremely flexible. Write about why you gave yourself that ranking.

_____

_____

_____

_____

_____

_____

_____

_____

_____

_____

Subtle Connection Neurologist Shekar Raman says that even subtle gestures, such as a hug, a pat on the back, or a friendly handshake, stimulate the reward center in the central nervous system. Understated gestures of connection with another person have a big impact on our psyche, inducing feelings of happiness and joy.

Today Reflect on the last few subtle gestures extended to you by another person and write about what those connections felt like.

➤ **You can benefit equally whether you are the person making the subtle gesture or the one receiving it. If you're the initiator, you can add this to tomorrow's list of random acts of kindness.**

_____

_____

_____

_____

_____

_____

_____

_____

Random Acts of Kindness As we saw in Week 2/Day 7, Sonja Lyubomirsky discovered that consolidating five to six random acts of kindness into one day created higher levels of happiness in study participants; their happiness was amplified by this intentional activity. The participants also had increased feelings of generosity, which contributed to a more positive self-image.

Today Commit to administering five to six random acts of kindness today, no matter how trivial or mundane they may appear on the surface. Quickly jot down a list of what you can do today. You're welcome to add to this list as your day progresses. The point is to be intentional about this practice.

_____

_____

_____

_____

_____

_____

_____

_____

Step by Step Millard Fuller, the founder of Habitat for Humanity, is believed to have said, "It's easier to act your way into a new way of thinking than to think your way into a new way of acting."

Today Write about what this quote means to you.

_____

_____

_____

_____

_____

_____

_____

_____

_____

_____

_____

_____

There's a Difference Self-esteem and self-acceptance are different. Self-esteem is how you value yourself, while self-acceptance is the ability to embrace all parts of yourself. It's unconditional.

Today Write about a part of yourself that you'd like to be more accepting of.

_____

_____

_____

_____

_____

_____

_____

_____

_____

_____

_____

_____

_____

Emotional Resilience Trait #4 Resilient people practice acceptance, note the experts at HeartMath. In this context, consider acceptance as the ability to avoid trying to control things you cannot change.

Today Write about a time when you struggled with trying to control an unchangeable situation or a time when you were willing to let go of control. In either case, what did you learn about yourself?

_____

_____

_____

_____

_____

_____

_____

_____

_____

_____

_____

Replacing "Forever" We may think that our mistakes, flaws, or stumbles are mortal sins or failures. Take a moment to consider this bit of wisdom attributed to elite runner Jon Sinclair: "Failure is a bruise, not a tattoo." Eventually the bruise fades. It might be sore for a bit, but eventually it goes away.

Today Make a list below of three or four mistakes or failures that may continue to make you uncomfortable. To the right of this list, write *This is not a permanent mark on my life. The pain will fade away.*

➤ **You may want to put these statements on sticky notes on your bathroom mirror to remind you that any current state of discomfort is only temporary.**

_____

_____

_____

_____

_____

_____

_____

_____

Derailed Impulses Regularly practicing gratitude fosters patience, which also informs the impulse not to make a poor choice, like overeating. "Gratitude replenishes willpower," says cognitive scientist Susan Peirce Thompson.

Today Write about your current state of willpower.

_____

_____

_____

_____

_____

_____

_____

_____

_____

_____

_____

_____

_____

Rewriting the Past We all wish we could have a redo at some point. However, that's simply not a reality. As you replace your old neuron patterns of coping with disappointment with more positive strategies, the history of your past becomes less charged; it just recedes into the background.

Today Reflect on a past experience that no longer holds a charge for you. Write about the transition point that created that release of negative emotions.

_____

_____

_____

_____

_____

_____

_____

_____

_____

_____

_____

_____

Gaining Optimism Dr. Fred Luskin, director of the Stanford Forgiveness Project, found that forgiveness positively impacts those who have experienced a severely traumatic event or loss. Those who have been taught forgiveness are less angry and stressed overall. Instead, they are able to embrace a more optimistic approach to life and show more compassion and increased resilience.

Today Consider someone you may still feel anger toward. Write about what it would take to forgive that person.

_____

_____

_____

_____

_____

_____

_____

_____

_____

_____

Commonality After any trauma or loss, the focus on human connection with loved ones becomes an essential ingredient toward healing, states educator and researcher Dr. Pauline Boss in her book *Loss, Trauma, and Resilience*. There is a power in bonding with others.

Today Write about a time when your loved ones helped you heal from a trauma or loss.

_____

_____

_____

_____

_____

_____

_____

_____

_____

_____

_____

Date_____

Staying Connected A simple nod or a "hello" to others is a way to stay engaged with those around you. It supports both the giver and receiver of the gesture.

Today Write about how it felt when someone acknowledged you with an unexpected "hello."

_____

_____

_____

_____

_____

_____

_____

_____

_____

_____

_____

Overlooked Health Benefit Oxytocin has a number of health benefits, including protecting your heart, reducing inflammation, and reducing signs of aging. Simple gestures of kindness, such as a smile, a kind word to others, or offering a helping hand, may just be our fountain of youth.

Today Write about one person whom you can focus on and gently shower with kindness today.

_____

_____

_____

_____

_____

_____

_____

_____

_____

_____

Imprinting a Memory In his autobiography, Benjamin Franklin noted that he found it helpful to keep a journal where he tracked his daily routines, writing that "The precept of Order [requires] that every part of my business should have its allotted time . . . for the twenty-four hours of a natural day."

Today Write about something positive you've learned in your life through repetition and routine.

➤ **Also, get ready for tomorrow's gratitude list!**

_____

_____

_____

_____

_____

_____

_____

_____

_____

_____

_____

Sleepless Somewhere The next time you find yourself wor-
rying, nervous, or fretting over something you cannot control,
try Dr. Susan Peirce Thompson's remedy of focusing on gratitude by putting pen to paper.

Today Write down three moments from today that make you
feel grateful.

_____

_____

_____

_____

_____

_____

_____

_____

_____

_____

_____

_____

_____

Gaining Insights Have you forgotten that you're amazing? We all do at times. Today, I really just want you to practice acceptance of yourself. Think about your amazing gifts and talents. Even if you've only listed one, it's one that makes you uniquely you. My sense of humor is one of my gifts. I may never be a stand-up comic, but my humor puts people at ease. It helps me lighten up a tense situation, and it aids in my not taking myself so seriously.

Today Write about one of your talents or gifts and how it serves you in your life or with other people.

_____

_____

_____

_____

_____

_____

_____

_____

_____

Mind-Changing Multiple studies have shown that gratitude induces pro-social behavior. Keeping a gratitude journal is enough to make you more likely to help others with their problems and offer them emotional support.

Today Write about how exercising gratitude affects your own life. For example, have you found yourself possibly offering more emotional support to people you are engaged with?

_____

_____

_____

_____

_____

_____

_____

_____

_____

_____

_____

Grinding It Out Hustling or chasing to "get it done" causes burnout. It is the antithesis of being resilient; you can't bounce back when you're flat on the floor. The remedy, according to Dr. Emma Seppälä, is a three-step process, starting with slowing down.

Today Write about where you may be experiencing burnout in your life. What would it feel like if you could slow down one single part of your day just a little bit?

_____

_____

_____

_____

_____

_____

_____

_____

_____

_____

_____

Swinging Doors There is a saying that when one door closes, another opens. Perhaps another way to consider this wisdom is that you can choose to close whatever door you like and open a different one.

Today Write about a door you'd like to close. Then consider what door you'd like to open.

➤ **Making it a deliberate decision sets a powerful intention.**

_____

_____

_____

_____

_____

_____

_____

_____

_____

_____

Change It Up James Clear suggests flipping judgmental self-talk by inserting a statement of hope. A couple of examples: "I really screwed up this time, but I have the opportunity to make this better." "I've failed, but I'm not the only one who ever has." "I'm completely devastated, but I know I can recover from this."

Today Write a handful of reframing statements that you can use in your current situation.

➤ **There is always a chance to recover, rebound, and rally!**

_____

_____

_____

_____

_____

_____

_____

_____

_____

_____

Hidden Strength I've watched women navigate cancer treatment and the deaths of loved ones. I've witnessed them rebuild their lives after floods, fires, divorces, and job losses. There is one common thread: Each woman told me they never knew they possessed the inner strength to overcome such challenges. Former First Lady Eleanor Roosevelt's words on this subject always make me laugh a little because they are so true: "Women are like tea bags. You never know how strong they are until they're in hot water."

Today Write about your inner strength.

_____

_____

_____

_____

_____

_____

_____

_____

_____

_____

Losing Something or Someone Grief is the reaction to the loss of anything significant in your life. It is a natural and normal human response. Loss is not limited to death; it can also include the ending of a relationship, a job, or a financial opportunity, to name a few.

Today Write about the natural grief response you may be having as the result of a recent loss.

_____

_____

_____

_____

_____

_____

_____

_____

_____

_____

Allow Some Space When we allow ourselves to sit silently, our inner voice offers wisdom, comfort, and guidance. "All profound things and emotions of things are preceded and attended by silence," wrote author Herman Melville.

Today Write the word *silence* below. Then just sit in silence for the next five minutes. Afterward, write about how this made you feel.

➤ You can find five minutes of silence at almost any time, any place.

_____

_____

_____

_____

_____

_____

_____

_____

_____

Reconnecting Psychiatrist Ralph Ryback suggests connecting with projects or people that make you feel as if you have a purpose. This can help you overcome the effects of any type of loss.

Today Write about one project or group that makes you feel connected to something good in your world.

_____

_____

_____

_____

_____

_____

_____

_____

_____

_____

_____

_____

_____

Laugh Therapy Belly-aching laughter is a quick way to release stress and lower cortisol levels, found Dr. William F. Fry of Stanford University. A long-time friend of my family died several years ago after struggling with cancer, leaving his wife of more than fifty years grief-stricken. Her family rallied around her in support, but the best medicine was making her laugh—really hard and often. When she laughed from the bottom of her soul, the weight of the years melted away and her depression began to lift. The aging from being her husband's caretaker softened; she actually began to look younger and have more energy, and was able to look forward to the next chapter of her life. Some people cry away their pain, while others laugh to release the stress. It's a personal choice.

Today Write about a time when you or someone you love experienced the remarkable healing effects of laughter.

_____

_____

_____

_____

_____

_____

_____

Happy Chemicals One of the best ways, in my opinion, to release more of the feel-good hormone oxytocin is to get a massage. Daily. Yes, daily. Practice self-massage, or trade massages with your partner. Building the habit of stimulating your oxytocin, writes Dr. Loretta Graziano Breuning in *Habits of a Happy Brain*, creates the ability to always access that pleasurable chemical release.

Today When was your last massage? Write about how it made you feel afterward.

_____

_____

_____

_____

_____

_____

_____

_____

_____

_____

Happy Feet Reflexology is a form of massage and acupressure applied to the feet or hands. This is another way to receive or give yourself a massage. Either way, oxytocin is stimulated.

Today Write about how it feels to have a foot massage after a long day. Even one that you give yourself counts.

_____

_____

_____

_____

_____

_____

_____

_____

_____

_____

_____

_____

_____

Losing Touch Isn't Forever According to Liggy Webb, author and founding director of the Learning Architect, the cornerstone of our very existence is our connection with others. Devoting time, energy, and attention to building strong relationships is one of our most valuable resilience skills. Have you noticed that we've been spending a considerable amount of time on this topic?

Today Write about a person with whom you have lost touch who has meant a lot to you. Send them an e-mail or text today to reconnect.

_____

_____

_____

_____

_____

_____

_____

_____

_____

_____

Impacting Others Communicate clearly and concisely. The goal of communication is to be understood, not just to speak.

Today Write about someone with whom you've recently had an unclear exchange. Think about where the breakdown may have occurred in your ability to convey your point of view.

➤ **Maybe this is an opportunity to repair that exchange through a helping of unexpected kindness.**

_____

_____

_____

_____

_____

_____

_____

_____

_____

_____

_____

_____

Listen with Your Eyes Give the person you are speaking with your complete attention. This means keeping your eyes on their eyes and not on your devices. Deeper connection with others stimulates the "love" hormone, which produces a calmer, more connected state.

Today Write about your level of comfort in making and keeping eye contact with others.

_____

_____

_____

_____

_____

_____

_____

_____

_____

_____

_____

Random Acts of Kindness Long-term happiness is fostered by helping others. It is a gift for both the receiver and the giver. There's a famous Chinese proverb related to this.

> *If you want happiness for an hour, take a nap.*
>
> *If you want happiness for a day, go fishing.*
>
> *If you want happiness for a month, get married.*
>
> *If you want happiness for a year, inherit a fortune.*
>
> *If you want happiness for a lifetime, help somebody else.*

Today Consider who may need a helping hand and write about one or two small "gifts" you can give that person.

_____

_____

_____

_____

_____

_____

_____

_____

Laughter Tip #1 Immunologist Dr. Lee S. Berk conducted studies showing that when we laugh, the pituitary glands release their own opiates, which suppress pain. Being able to find the humor in our missteps, disappointments, or sadness could be the key to bouncing back more quickly.

Today Make a list of the top five shows or comedians that make you laugh. At the end of your list, go back and circle one that you can watch tonight.

_____

_____

_____

_____

_____

_____

_____

_____

_____

_____

_____

Laughter Tip #2 Dr. Berk's studies also indicated that laughter can increase the production of immune cells and their ability to accelerate the body's natural anticarcinogenic responses. This means a healthier you.

Today Write about types of activities that make you smile or giggle. List three of them and decide on one that you'll do this week. If you cannot decide, simply start with a walk outside in the fresh air. It's not a sprint or a marathon—just a stroll to make you smile.

_____

_____

_____

_____

_____

_____

_____

_____

_____

_____

_____

Emotional Resilience Trait #5 Those who are resilient know when to ask for help, according to HeartMath. You are not helpless, but sometimes it's a good idea to enlist the assistance of others.

Today Write about a time when you know you should have asked for help but didn't. Why did you choose to struggle?

_____

_____

_____

_____

_____

_____

_____

_____

_____

_____

_____

_____

Stay Open A willingness to be vulnerable provides an opening to discover new ways of resolving emotional and situational issues. Dr. Brené Brown has said that "Vulnerability [is] uncertainty, risk, and emotional exposure. . . . To be human is to be in vulnerability."

Today Write about a time when you made yourself vulnerable to another person. How did that feel? What was the result?

_____

_____

_____

_____

_____

_____

_____

_____

_____

_____

_____

_____

Productive Banter Parents can help their children build resilience and problem-solving skills by brainstorming with them. Adults also find brainstorming together a productive way to find solutions. If you're feeling stuck, then it's time to find a partner or partners to brainstorm with: people who can ask you objective questions to help you find your answers.

Today Make a note of who could help you brainstorm and why they are your choice.

_____

_____

_____

_____

_____

_____

_____

_____

_____

_____

_____

Gaining Awareness Noticing and marking positive points in your life are part of creating a healthy habit and acceptance practice. Psychology professor and author Barbara Fredrickson advises that "It helps to be able to develop an eye for the positive, to even go through your day asking, 'Is this one of those [positive] things?'"

Today Write about something you will have the opportunity to experience that could lead you to ask this question. It could be a stimulating social setting, a productive meeting, coffee with a friend, a rewarding exercise class—anything that emphasizes the positive.

_____

_____

_____

_____

_____

_____

_____

_____

_____

_____

Building Relationships Daniel Lumera, president of the International School of Forgiveness, has found that forgiveness promotes happier, healthier, and more trusting relationships.

Today Write about a relationship you feel very safe within, and where you could offer and accept forgiveness to/from that person.

_____

_____

_____

_____

_____

_____

_____

_____

_____

_____

_____

_____

Cap It Off In his book *Extreme Productivity*, author and strategic management expert Robert Pozen suggests capping all meetings at one hour. He contends that shorter meetings are more efficient and that after an hour, meeting participants become too impatient or tired to productively contribute or pay attention.

Today Write about how you could use this advice to make your appointments, personally and professionally, more efficient, to give yourself more energy during the day.

➤ **Having healthy boundaries around your time is one way to insure that you're not completely drained.**

_____

_____

_____

_____

_____

_____

_____

_____

False Emergencies Pozen states that most people find, when pressed, that they do not need to work late on a regular basis. At times there may be a legitimate emergency, of course. Still, he encourages spending a couple hours a day to reconnect with family and friends.

Today Write an honest assessment about how much you work.

_____

_____

_____

_____

_____

_____

_____

_____

_____

_____

_____

_____

Good Feelings Empathy is engagement and understanding without blame or trying to fix a situation. The end result is how you made another person feel. One of the most empathetic people I ever worked for became a lifelong friend. She always made me feel strong, smart, and fully supported, no matter what.

Today Write about the person whose empathy has positively impacted your life.

_____

_____

_____

_____

_____

_____

_____

_____

_____

_____

_____

Human Contact Touch has proven to lower blood pressure and cortisol levels. A study at the University of North Carolina found that people who hugged their significant others frequently, even if just briefly, reaped the benefits with lower blood pressure and heart rates.

Today Remember the hugs you've experienced from family or friends. Write about that warm, comforting experience.

_____

_____

_____

_____

_____

_____

_____

_____

_____

_____

Connecting Having a partner who expresses gratitude creates a stronger feeling of connection in a relationship.

Today Write a thank-you note to your partner or loved one expressing your gratitude. Consider this a part of the acts-of-random-kindness habit you're developing.

_____

_____

_____

_____

_____

_____

_____

_____

_____

_____

_____

_____

_____

_____

Your Most Excellent Self In my work with women, we talk a lot about strengths. But the world seems to talk more about weaknesses and how that's where we need to focus. We all need to hone skills, both personally and professionally, but if we constantly focus on the negative, it's very self-defeating; you may hear that little voice of doubt in your mind sneaking in. Stanford University sociologist Shelly J. Correll found in a career-based study that women judge themselves more harshly than men judge themselves. Beating yourself up—whether over work or anything else—is a total waste of time, my friend. So let's knock that off!

Today Make a rapid-fire list of the strengths, talents, and gifts for which you're most grateful. GO! Don't stop! GO!

_____

_____

_____

_____

_____

_____

_____

_____

Epiphany Check-In Take a moment to consider all you have learned over the past few months. What are the key lessons that stand out to you?

Today Write about what these are for you. Choose three to five and write about why they stand out.

_____

_____

_____

_____

_____

_____

_____

_____

_____

_____

_____

_____

_____

_____

Laugh It Off Psychologists found that people who can laugh at themselves may find solutions easier to come by. Psychologist and laughter researcher Rod Martin theorizes that laughter accelerates the heartbeat, increasing the oxygen supply to the brain and thereby improving mental performance. Allowing yourself to crack up over your foibles also helps you have a better attitude toward life in general—and makes others around you more comfortable. For example, during a presentation to a roomful of people, my colleague Susan stumbled while wearing three-inch heels, almost falling. Instead of panicking she began to laugh and make a joke about her clumsiness. The group followed suit. It lightened the mood, and her ability to roll with the punches was noted as a positive attribute.

Today Think about a time when you were able to laugh at yourself while in a tough spot. Write about how others reacted to your use of humor as a way to defuse the situation.

_____

_____

_____

_____

_____

_____

New Dreams As the old adage advises, "When one door closes, another one opens." Your life has limitless opportunities. Be courageous. Walk through the next door.

Today Write about whatever new doors or opportunities you see in front of you. Or write about the doors you would like to see.

_____

_____

_____

_____

_____

_____

_____

_____

_____

_____

_____

_____

_____

We All Fall Down A popular quote apocryphally attributed to Winston Churchill said, "Success is not final, failure is not fatal: it is the courage to continue that counts." In short, by summoning your courage, you can write a new chapter in your life. It's just a matter of being courageous enough to do so.

Today Write about what a brand new chapter in your life could look like.

_____

_____

_____

_____

_____

_____

_____

_____

_____

_____

_____

_____

Finding Beauty We are all imperfectly perfect human beings. Our flaws are what make us unique individuals. It is also the stuff that forms our character.

Today Write about one perceived imperfection you have and how it has or still does serve you to your benefit.

_____

_____

_____

_____

_____

_____

_____

_____

_____

_____

_____

_____

Perfection Is a Myth Imagine the person you admire most. What idiosyncrasy, flaw, or imperfection do they possess? It could be a physical trait, a character flaw, or an emotional shortfall. Does that matter to you?

Today Write about how this understanding of the person may be an equalizing factor for you. Does it help you relate to that person more or less when you recognize their imperfections?

_____

_____

_____

_____

_____

_____

_____

_____

_____

_____

Dare to Be When asked what makes one person more resilient than another, Charles Hunt, founder of the Audacity
Firm, said, "[It is] an irrational hope that tomorrow will be
better than today."

Today What does the ability to have an "irrational hope" mean
to you?

_____

_____

_____

_____

_____

_____

_____

_____

_____

_____

_____

_____

Checklist University of Calabar, Nigeria, lecturers Dr. Emeka Ekeke and Dr. Ubong Eyo detail hope as having several key elements:

* *It is attainable with a level of certainty.*

* *It can bring only goodness into your life.*

* *It is perceived as difficult to obtain.*

* *It presents uncertainty of realization.*

* *It lies beyond the control of the individual.*

Today Which of the above elements resonate with you right now when you think about hope, and why?

_____

_____

_____

_____

_____

_____

_____

_____

Making Choices Carl Jung reminds us that you are not what happened to you. No matter what the event, challenge, or mountain, you have the opportunity to make choices in your life for a positive direction—regardless of what's come before.

Today What from your past is still defining you?

_____

_____

_____

_____

_____

_____

_____

_____

_____

_____

_____

_____

Are We in a Relationship? I'm often asked what constitutes a relationship. It's a bigger mystery than you may realize. Psychologists Harry Mills and Mark Dombeck offer the following structure to gain clarity:

* *Relationships require a give-and-take of ideas and feelings.*

* *Relationships require reciprocity.*

* *Ongoing attention and nurturing are musts.*

Today Consider your closest relationships. Do they have the above characteristics to varying degrees?

_____

_____

_____

_____

_____

_____

_____

_____

_____

Taking a Stand Drs. Mills and Dombeck suggest choosing quality over quantity when it comes to building resilient relationships. This goes both ways.

Today Write about how you are making the choice to be a higher-quality friend, partner, lover, or employee.

_____

_____

_____

_____

_____

_____

_____

_____

_____

_____

_____

_____

Socially Connected Resilience researcher Elliot Friedman concluded consistently engaging in the world through meaningful activities—being socially connected to others—boosts resilience by promoting feelings of purpose and meaning.

Today Write about the activities you routinely engage in with others that feel meaningful and full of purpose for you.

_____

_____

_____

_____

_____

_____

_____

_____

_____

_____

_____

_____

_____

Powerful Gestures In his book *Life, the Truth, and Being Free*, author and motivational speaker Steve Maraboli advises, "Give yourself entirely to those around you. Be generous with your blessings. A kind gesture can reach a wound that only compassion can heal."

Today Write about the positive effects that giving to others has had on your or another person's emotional well-being.

_____

_____

_____

_____

_____

_____

_____

_____

_____

_____

_____

_____

Spacing It Out A daily routine can sometimes feel boring. Yet routines can have many subtle benefits. According to the experts at SkilledatLife.com, repetition creates structure around your most valuable asset: your time. It helps you prioritize your day and remove the need to exert willpower in certain situations. This paves the way for momentum and focus to happen naturally in your life.

Today Write about your current routine or one you'd like to put into practice. If you already have one, what adjustments could you make to streamline your day?

➤ Prepare for your monthly act of kindness check-in. It's coming up tomorrow. Consider what you can do.

_____

_____

_____

_____

_____

_____

_____

_____

The Time-Release Effect Kindness has a time-release component to it. On his blog, Dr. David R. Hamilton cites a recent UK study that found that *doing* good can improve your ability to *feel* good—and the effects can last as long as 24 days. In those who are in the 18 to 24 age group, the effects can last for an astounding 34 days. This feeling is called the "Helper's High," a term coined by social change expert Allan Luks.

Today Write about what kindnesses you can offer this week that will promote your own "helper's high."

_____

_____

_____

_____

_____

_____

_____

_____

_____

_____

Shoulda, Coulda, Woulda When we don't forgive ourselves for doing—or not doing—something in the past, we risk stepping into a self-blaming, self-perpetuating state of *obsessive regret*, states psychologist Robert Karen. Not respecting your past choices or past blunders can put you in a depressive hole, says Karen, unable to forgive yourself or allow yourself to explore and make mistakes.

Today Write about a *shoulda, coulda, woulda* you may have experienced or continue to experience regret over. Can you let it go and forgive yourself? If not now, when?

_____

_____

_____

_____

_____

_____

_____

_____

Heart-Healthy Laughter Researchers found that laughter decreases cortisol, which contributes to heart disease and hypertension. Your heart needs laughter to stay healthy.

Today Write about a relative, a friend, or a group of friends who always makes you smile or laugh. Make plans to see them in the next two weeks.

_____

_____

_____

_____

_____

_____

_____

_____

_____

_____

_____

_____

Emotional Resilience Trait #6 Those who are resilient, according to HeartMath, have impeccable discernment in knowing how to support others, including when to listen, when to intervene, and when to step away. They continually refine how to manage this delicate balance.

Today Write about an exchange in which you were able to support a friend or a family member.

_____

_____

_____

_____

_____

_____

_____

_____

_____

_____

_____

Deeper Connection Supporting others and offering reassurance that they can overcome a difficult issue is a generous gift. Resolving the issue for them isn't necessary.

Today Write about someone in your life who may need your reassurance. How can you be there for them without trying to "fix" their situation?

_____

_____

_____

_____

_____

_____

_____

_____

_____

_____

_____

_____

Meaning and Momentum People generally feel a sense of purpose in their lives when they are able to contribute to another's life.

Today Write about an instance when you made a positive impact on someone.

_____

_____

_____

_____

_____

_____

_____

_____

_____

_____

_____

_____

_____

_____

Loving Your Past Holding love for your past means accepting whatever happened and however you reacted to it. It's what makes you who you are today—stronger, more self-aware, and full of empathy for others.

Today Write about a negative experience that provided you with great insights or lessons in your life.

_____

_____

_____

_____

_____

_____

_____

_____

_____

_____

_____

_____

_____

Most Need More It's as important to forgive as to be forgiven; the health benefits are the same. Forgiveness reduces anger, resentment, and hostility and replaces those negative feelings with compassion, empathy, and understanding. People who are more forgiving are more satisfied with their lives, experiencing less depression, anxiety, and stress. The Fetzer Institute found that 62 percent of American adults surveyed felt they needed more forgiveness in their lives.

Today Write about an apology you need to make to another person, or an apology that was given to you that you feel fully ready to accept.

_____

_____

_____

_____

_____

_____

_____

_____

_____

_____

Peaking Over the Edge Uncertainty and change can be the catalysts for stepping forward into uncharted waters. Neale Donald Walsch, author of the acclaimed spiritual book *Conversations with God*, reminds us that "Life begins at the end of your comfort zone."

Today Write about an area of your comfort zone that you know you need to release. What's holding you back?

_____

_____

_____

_____

_____

_____

_____

_____

_____

_____

_____

_____

Mindful Mantra In a moment of worry, concern, or plain fear, remind yourself, "It is just for this moment. It is not forever."

Today Write about a current concern. Take a deep breath. Then write out the above statement.

_____

_____

_____

_____

_____

_____

_____

_____

_____

_____

_____

_____

_____

Positive Mental State Overcoming stress has a lot to do with creating a positive mental attitude. Yesterday we touched on negative events being just a moment in time. This is a gentle reminder to use this technique when you become over-whelmed or start to feel stress creeping up on you.

Today Write about the effects you have experienced by deploying this technique. Remember: Practice makes perfect and routine builds your resilience muscles.

_____

_____

_____

_____

_____

_____

_____

_____

_____

_____

_____

Date_____   **Week 28 • Day 4**

Awareness Is Key Taking a moment to identify what it is that is bringing fear (and ultimately stress) into your life is paramount in being able to overcome it. Over the past few months we've touched on this topic in various ways. Have you noticed a pattern in regard to what causes your fears?

Today Write about a potential pattern (or patterns) you've noticed when it comes to feeling fearful or stressed out.

_____

_____

_____

_____

_____

_____

_____

_____

_____

_____

Pause Before Hitting Play Multiple studies have shown that patience comes from regularly practicing gratitude. The next time you are on the verge of making a rash decision, press pause and think of three good things that happened to you this week. Then take a deep breath and make your decision.

Today Take that pause and identify one consistently grateful thing that's in your life. Write it down.

➤ **Access this memory in times of overwhelm to help calm you.**

_____

_____

_____

_____

_____

_____

_____

_____

Being the One A quote attributed to R. Buckminster Fuller reads: "Never forget that you are one of a kind. Never forget that if there weren't any need for you in all your uniqueness to be on this earth, you wouldn't be here in the first place. And never forget, no matter how overwhelming life's challenges and problems seem to be, that one person can make a difference in the world. In fact, it is always because of one person that all the changes that matter in the world come about. So be that person."

Today Write about what this means in your life.

_____

_____

_____

_____

_____

_____

_____

_____

_____

Date_____   **Week 28 • Day 7**

Offering Thanks Our gratitude practice today will be about saying thank you to people. This seemingly simple acknowledgment of others goes a long way in strengthening your connection with them.

Today Make a list of three people you can say thank you to. It can be verbal or via e-mail, note card, or sticky note.

➤ **If you are a spiritual person, you can also say thank you to your divine director. That counts.**

_____

_____

_____

_____

_____

_____

_____

_____

_____

_____

_____

Date_____

The Love Hormone Oxytocin is associated with feelings of love and trust. Spending more time with family and friends whom you trust helps increase the oxytocin in your system.

Today Write about the trusting relationships in your life.

_____

_____

_____

_____

_____

_____

_____

_____

_____

_____

_____

_____

_____

_____

Just Feel It Who and what do you want to be today? The person who gets promoted? The person who is strong? The person who is kind in a difficult situation? Author Pamela Palladino Gold suggests you take a moment to consider what it might feel like to be that person.

Today Who do you want to be today? How do you feel about that person? What do you need in order to show up as that person today?

_____

_____

_____

_____

_____

_____

_____

_____

_____

_____

_____

Failing into It To "fail into" something is to learn from your mistakes and make corrections—it's a great way to reframe your feelings about the setbacks or stumbles you might encounter. Next time you'll do it or handle it better.

Today Write about a time when you felt like you were failing. What did you learn from the experience?

➤ Cut yourself a break—this is normal.

_____

_____

_____

_____

_____

_____

_____

_____

_____

_____

_____

Denial Creates Blind Spots A 2018 study at UCLA data scientist Jared Torre and neuroscientist Matthew Lieberman determined that acknowledging the origin of your stress enables the brain to move from an automatic reaction to a more conscious response, using the "affect labeling" technique. Dr. Lara Fielding, author of *Mastering Adulthood*, explains that first you turn inward and pinpoint what stressed you out, and then find a verbal label for the emotion, for example: *I am angry when this or that happened* or *I am annoyed with that person or this event.* This technique trains you to bypass a purely reactionary response to a stressor.

Today Write about a current stressor. Identify it. Give it a name. Be as specific as you can so that you become more aware of the true cause of that stress rather than allowing your brain to be reactive. Is it fear of loss? Do you feel threatened or afraid of the unknown? Does the situation make you feel insecure?

_____

_____

_____

_____

_____

_____

What Is Your Default? Building on yesterday's topic of stress, let's take another step in the process. Consider your default, knee-jerk reaction to that stressor you named. Some people have a drink, raid the fridge, or withdraw emotionally; others become overly emotional, defensive, or argumentative.

Today Write about how you react to stress. How has this reaction served you, and how has it hurt you? Consider both sides of the coin. There are pros and cons to everything we experience in life.

_____

_____

_____

_____

_____

_____

_____

_____

_____

_____

Seeing It Through Dr. Chan Hellman and Casey Gwinn, founder of the Family Justice Center movement, define hope as the belief that tomorrow will be better than today. By utilizing mental strategies (pathways or "waypower") and applying our agency (willpower) we can achieve our goals and make tomorrow happen.

Today Write about the waypower you'll utilize to make what you hope for come to be, such as specific decisions you will make or goal-setting tasks you will begin. Take baby steps if you need to. It's perfectly okay.

_____

_____

_____

_____

_____

_____

_____

_____

_____

Mitigating Trauma To date, there are about two thousand studies on the effects of hope in overcoming trauma. Dr. Hellman found that each and every one of these studies establishes hope as the best predictor of well-being.

Today Write about an experience when hopefulness helped you overcome a difficult situation.

_____

_____

_____

_____

_____

_____

_____

_____

_____

_____

_____

_____

Flipping Triggers When you laugh, author Marshall Brain explains, your brain produces an electrical wave that moves through five different brain regions via a circuit. However, other emotional responses are confined to specific regions. Research also shows that humans more easily retain memories and information associated with humor and laughter.

Today Write about a particular scenario that makes you laugh every time you think of it.

_____

_____

_____

_____

_____

_____

_____

_____

_____

_____

_____

_____

Deploy Your Tools We've been exploring the health benefits of laughter. Building a stronger you can help you bounce back from challenges. Sometimes all it takes is a smile. Literally. Consider this 1-2-3 sequence that you can deploy at any time:

1. Enjoy a bout of outright laughter; watch a video clip or listen to a podcast you know will make you laugh.

2. Connect with people who make you smile or laugh.

3. Move your body in a way that makes you smile: take a casual stroll, dance to your favorite song, or do some other easygoing activity.

Today Take a look at the calendar and find three days where you can enact this 1-2-3 process. How will you pursue each step? This will help put you in a cycle of healing your mind, heart, and body.

_____

_____

_____

_____

_____

_____

_____

Self-Care Basics Let's properly define self-care. According to experts at the American Psychiatric Association, self-care is "a multidimensional, multifaceted process of purposeful engagement in strategies that promote healthy functioning and enhance well-being." Those who engage in such activities experience feelings of calm and reassurance.

Today Write about the types of self-care that make you feel calm and reassured.

_____

_____

_____

_____

_____

_____

_____

_____

_____

_____

Paired Strategies Most self-care activities are interconnected. For example:

* *Meditation won't help if you're not sleeping enough.*

* *Working out won't help if you're eating poorly.*

We can all do just a little bit better in the self-care area. Remember, if you're not taking care of yourself, then you won't run at an optimal level to take care of others, work effectively, and make decisions with clarity.

Today Write about the *one* thing you can do to ramp up your self-care game.

_____

_____

_____

_____

_____

_____

_____

_____

_____

Setting Boundaries An often-overlooked form of self-care is the art of setting boundaries around your time. Without boundaries, burnout can become a very real problem. Work reinvention expert Sarah Kathleen Peck suggests working on any issue or assignment in segments lasting no longer than ninety minutes. Also, taking a five-minute break in between activities will increase your efficacy. Healthy, practical boundaries matter.

Today Write about an upcoming task or assignment. Break it down into ninety-minute segments on your calendar, without distractions. Then please plan something enjoyable to do afterward that will make you want to hold yourself to that ninety-minute framework. Rewards matter too!

_____

_____

_____

_____

_____

_____

_____

_____

Nature Cements the Need Dr. David R. Hamilton believes
that the reason kindness makes people happier is because it is
deeply embedded in your psyche. Kindness is reinforced two-
fold: It is natural to be helpful, and the chemical reaction in
our brains makes it so pleasant that we'll want to help again.

Today Write about the kindness you find yourself deploying
in a natural, spontaneous manner without really consider-
ing it.

_____

_____

_____

_____

_____

_____

_____

_____

_____

_____

_____

A Daily Boost Have you noticed that when you do something kind, you feel happier? A study by researchers at the University of Kent in Great Britain published in the *Journal of Social Psychology* confirmed that doing daily acts of kindness significantly boosts feelings of happiness and life satisfaction.

Today Write this simple question at the top of your page: *Did I make someone feel good today?* Now answer it. If your answer is yes, then you've completed your act of random kindness.

_____

_____

_____

_____

_____

_____

_____

_____

_____

_____

_____

_____

Autopilot A 2012 *Vanity Fair* article quotes former President Barack Obama as saying, "You'll see I wear only gray or blue suits. I'm trying to pare down decisions. I don't want to make decisions about what I'm eating or wearing. Because I have too many other decisions to make. . . . You need to focus your decision-making energy." This is the method the president used to reduce decision fatigue: putting certain aspects of his life on autopilot.

Today Write about three things you can put on autopilot in your life to reduce your decision fatigue.

_____

_____

_____

_____

_____

_____

_____

_____

Know Your Limit For more than a decade, my mother cared for my father as he declined into the depths of Alzheimer's disease, which would eventually end his life. She was a rock, but at times she experienced periods when she wasn't able to make decisions. It wasn't because of her age or the emotional aspect of the decision; it was simply because she'd maxed out her capacity to make yet another decision, at least in that moment.

Today Who are the one or two people in your life who can help you when you become overwhelmed? How can they help?

_____

_____

_____

_____

_____

_____

_____

_____

_____

_____

Emotional Resilience Trait #7 Engaging with other positive people, the seventh trait listed by HeartMath, is a sign of a resilient person. Like attracts like, and positive support creates a strong platform to build relationships on. Negativity, pessimism, and criticism drain your resources.

Today Make a list of those positive, uplifting people in your inner circle. What aspects of their positive expressions do you appreciate most?

_____

_____

_____

_____

_____

_____

_____

_____

_____

_____

_____

Ripe Fruit As said by author William P. Young in his best-selling book *The Shack*, "Trust is the fruit of a relationship in which you know you are loved." Trust is an essential ingredient in all relationships. Each person is deserving of a level of trust.

Today Reflect on a relationship you have with someone you do not fully trust compared with another relationship built on deep trust. Write about how they are different.

_____

_____

_____

_____

_____

_____

_____

_____

_____

_____

_____

Grudge Power The love hormone oxytocin is a wonderful by-product of feeling loved, trusted, and connected to those around you. But harboring the opposite of these emotions—feeling angry, mistrusting, and resentful—can be toxic. Studies have shown that levels of cortisol, the natural stress hormone, were heightened in those who harbored a grudge or resentment against another person.

Today What grudges are you still holding on to that may be limiting your oxytocin levels? Is it time to release that stockpile of cortisol through forgiveness?

_____

_____

_____

_____

_____

_____

_____

_____

_____

_____

Overriding the Past Your brain can be trained or retrained to learn new coping skills. Linda Graham, psychotherapist and author of *Bouncing Back*, explains that deliberately engaging in thoughts of gratitude, self-compassion, and acceptance creates new, more resilient ways of responding to life events. Additionally, you can recondition memories of bad situations by juxtaposing them in your mind with positive outcomes or even imagined scenarios. This builds new neurological pathways that will eventually override the existing experiences.

Today Write about an experience you can give yourself to create that new positive memory you want to be ingrained in your brain.

➤ **Consider different apps or music to help with this process.**

_____

_____

_____

_____

_____

_____

_____

_____

A Personal Commitment There are times when someone may not offer the apology that you'd like. This is not something you can force. Mayo Clinic researchers suggest that you practice empathy and try seeing the situation from the other person's point of view.

Today Write about a time when you really thought you deserved an apology but never got it. How did that affect your relationship? Are you still walking around with that feeling?

_____

_____

_____

_____

_____

_____

_____

_____

_____

_____

_____

Risk Being Seen Dr. Brené Brown offers insight into vulnerability by reminding us that there are no perfect experiences in life; we have to be willing to show up, be seen, and be all in—even when we can't control the outcome.

Today Is there a scenario in your life where you could gain something by showing more vulnerability—by showing up and being all in? Write about that situation and what you would risk by actually being seen.

_____

_____

_____

_____

_____

_____

_____

_____

_____

_____

_____

Lean on Me Even the world's happiest people sometimes need to lean on someone for help. When they do so, they are building resilience.

Today Write about an incident when someone helped you traverse a challenge. How did their support make you feel? Did asking for help change your relationship?

_____

_____

_____

_____

_____

_____

_____

_____

_____

_____

_____

_____

Colorful Meditation Mandala coloring books have become healing tools in medical communities. Mandalas (Sanskrit for *circle*) are traditional, intricate circular designs; in Tibetan Buddhist traditions they are considered diagrams of the cosmos. Coloring mandalas is a form of meditation that helps you to focus and to express your creative side, says wellness journalist Cathy Wong. Best of all, no special skill set is required. It has been used to reduce stress in children, help relax people dealing with critical illnesses, or even support those seeking to stop smoking.

Today Write about the idea of coloring as a meditation.

➤ **Mandala coloring books are easily found online or in bookstores.**

_____

_____

_____

_____

_____

_____

_____

_____

Sometimes a Six-Year-Old Knows Best My little neighbor intuitively always knew the best way to help me come back down to planet Earth after a stressful day. Many times over the years of my husband's sickness, I needed her help. She'd plop down her coloring books, crayons, markers, and stickers and then explain what all the stickers were and how to use them. She would instruct me to color a butterfly. By the end of our "session," I would be smiling and laughing as we compared masterpieces. It was just the medicine I needed.

Today Who are the kids in your life who would be thrilled to have you color with them? Your kids? Nieces or nephews? Grandchildren? Godchildren? Your best friend's kids? Next time you see them, suggest a coloring session where you can both have fun and connect.

➤ **Tomorrow is gratitude day!**

_____

_____

_____

_____

_____

_____

Gratitude Download Are you getting the hang of this? It's actually rewarding, isn't it? Take a deep breath and consider people, places, and things that fill you with a sense of gratitude.

Today Write about three things you feel grateful for in your life and how they affect you.

_____

_____

_____

_____

_____

_____

_____

_____

_____

_____

_____

_____

Sensory Journey Experts have concluded that sense of smell is strongly linked to memory. There is nothing in the world like the smell of something pleasant to take us back to a specific moment in time.

Today What scent brings you back to a happy place? Pause for a moment, take a deep breath, and imagine inhaling that calming, happy feeling. If you can, try to re-create the scent as a quick boost.

➤ Flowers, essential oils, a cake in the oven, the smell of the ocean, or a log burning in the fireplace are just some examples you might consider.

_____

_____

_____

_____

_____

_____

_____

_____

_____

Ensuring Your Zs Those who make a habit of marking what they're grateful for prior to bedtime sleep better. Dr. Emma Seppälä and other researchers conclude that these happy, positive thoughts help quiet negative ones, which can keep you tossing and turning.

Today Write about how your practice of gratitude may be affecting your sleep.

_____

_____

_____

_____

_____

_____

_____

_____

_____

_____

_____

Antiflu Researchers in McGill University's psychology department found that listening to music increases levels of the antibody immunoglobulin A, a crucial part of the immune function that inhibits the growth of certain bacteria and viruses. Enjoying music actually makes you a stronger, healthier person!

Today Write about how you can integrate more music into your day.

_____

_____

_____

_____

_____

_____

_____

_____

_____

_____

Keep It Simple Registered dietician Natalia Bailey Groat explains that keeping your meals simple will make it easier to eat a healthy diet of fruits, vegetables, lean proteins, and whole grains, which can minimize inflammation caused by stress.

Today Write about the easiest healthy choice you can make today to help your body feel good.

_____

_____

_____

_____

_____

_____

_____

_____

_____

_____

_____

Toss Out Perfection Groat also believes that perfection isn't necessary. Allow yourself to indulge in your favorite foods—just not on a regular basis. The objective is to feel good. Allow your body to handle any stress you may be experiencing without adding pressure from a too-restrictive diet.

Today Write about your one special food or beverage indulgence and why it makes you feel happy or comforted.

_____

_____

_____

_____

_____

_____

_____

_____

_____

_____

_____

Beyond Lack of Mental Clarity Sleep deprivation releases the hunger hormone, ghrelin, and lessens the release of the satiety hormone, leptin. Bottom line: Lack of sleep not only affects your mental clarity, decision-making, and resilience; it also affects your waistline.

Today Write about the last food splurge you had after a sleepless night.

_____

_____

_____

_____

_____

_____

_____

_____

_____

_____

_____

Winding Down Presleep rituals become a habit when utilized on a regular basis. It can be taking a shower, listening to music, shutting off the TV at a certain time, deep breathing, reading something uplifting, or journaling. The goal is to end the day and separate anything unpleasant or distressing from your sacred sleep time.

Today Write about the presleep ritual you currently have or would like to put in place.

_____

_____

_____

_____

_____

_____

_____

_____

_____

_____

_____

Finding Hope To be hopeful means that you are willing to project into the future things that are unseen—desires, goals, hopeful scenarios. In other words, it can be described as surrounding yourself with the improbable anticipation that life will get better.

Today Write about what you're projecting into the future with your hopefulness.

_____

_____

_____

_____

_____

_____

_____

_____

_____

_____

_____

Talk to Yourself "Sometimes we need to tell ourselves what to think when our minds start to tell us things we don't need to hear," shares resilience expert Charles Hunt. "That you can and will overcome and succeed. . . . That with the proper perspective and a positive attitude, we have power. That life is easier when you're prepared. And just because you can't plan for everything doesn't mean you can't be ready for something. That perspective sometimes requires partnership and perseverance."

Today How can you encourage yourself to overcome whatever trauma or setback you've experienced?

_____

_____

_____

_____

_____

_____

_____

_____

_____

Knowing When It's Time to Let Go In 2008, I decided to leave my corporate career and start a business. I was elated! What I didn't expect was the impact that losing my corporate identity had on me. After leaving a decades-old career, I felt like I had lost my place in the world and my reason for being. Looking back, it took me more than a year to grieve my loss. At times, it was heartbreaking and very confusing—after all, no one had died. Then I was reminded that a part of me had. It was a part of myself that I needed to let go of in order to move forward and evolve into a new, different identity. The process of renewal took as long as it needed to take.

Today Write about a loss of identity in your life. What caused it? How did you feel? Are you still grieving?

_____

_____

_____

_____

_____

_____

_____

_____

Completion While many people try to immediately replace that which they have lost, grief expert John W. James points out when a spouse or a loved one passes away, it's important to complete the relationship that you've lost before moving on. An example of completion could mean saying what you've always wanted to but never did. This could be done alone in a quiet place by yourself or as a written letter to the departed. James's point is that you should try to complete what has felt incomplete in that relationship so you can move on.

Today Consider someone you may be grieving. Write them a letter or make a list of things you wish you had said or done with them.

➤ **We have all lost someone we loved. It's okay if your completion is for someone you lost many years ago.**

_____

_____

_____

_____

_____

_____

_____

Mind Wide Open Dani DiPirro, noted positivity blogger and author of *The Positively Present Guide to Life*, suggests that having an open mind opens you up to new experiences and ideas that could change your perception of the world around you. Consider someone you met who provided insight into a situation you may have never considered. These encounters are a gift. They allow us to let go of preconceived notions and explore options we never knew existed.

Today Write about a point of view that gave you a new take on the world around you.

_____

_____

_____

_____

_____

_____

_____

_____

_____

_____

Fresh Air Without varying perspectives, we can become stale or set in our ways. However, new people in your life can bring a breath of fresh air. They can validate your current view or provide you with an alternate, updated view that is in alignment with the positivity you want to infuse into your world.

Today Write about a person you've met whose attitudes are completely opposite from yours, whether positive or negative. What have you learned from your experiences with them?

➤ Surround yourself with positive, uplifting people—always. Negativity and complacency will only bring you down.

_____

_____

_____

_____

_____

_____

_____

_____

Flipping the Switch Positive psychology pioneer Martin Seligman believes that developing a more optimistic approach to life challenges is part of building resilience. He says pessimists react to setbacks with three main explanatory styles:

* **Permanence:** *Pessimists view setbacks as permanent ("My friend never wants to see me again"), while optimists view them as temporary ("My friend is busy tonight").*

* **Pervasiveness:** *Pessimists overgeneralize ("I can't do anything right"); optimists view negative outcomes as contained to specific situations ("I'm not able to do this one thing").*

* **Personalization:** *Pessimists blame themselves for bad events ("I messed up because I'm useless"); optimists realize external events are in play ("I didn't get support I needed").*

Today Write two negative statements you've recently said or thought; then rewrite them in an optimistic style.

_____

_____

_____

_____

_____

_____

_____

Creatures of Habit Our habits are developed based on life experiences that create patterns. Negative thinking is, unfortunately, one of them. Consider yesterday's writing prompt and reflect on what you may now be able to see as a habitual pattern of negative thought. Do you see setbacks as lasting situations (permanence)? Do you consider aspects of life in blanket statements of good or bad (pervasiveness)? Or do you consistently blame yourself for everything (personalization)?

Today Identify the pessimistic habitual thought pattern you see running through your life. Is it personalization, pervasiveness, or permanence?

➤ Naming the habit makes it easier to identify how to defuse the pattern as it plays out on a daily basis. Use one or more of the optimistic styles to recraft those thoughts.

_____

_____

_____

_____

_____

_____

_____

Making It Automatic Because of our brain's neuroplasticity, repeating kind acts can create a good habit, concludes Terry Small. Embracing kindness as a daily practice makes it something you no longer need to think about. It just becomes part of who you are in the world.

Today Write about the kindness you can extend to yourself today. Start within. You also get to be a recipient of your random acts of kindness.

_____

_____

_____

_____

_____

_____

_____

_____

_____

_____

_____

_____

Heavy Lifting Taking a break is always a good idea—including taking one from your daily journaling. Instead of writing today, consider what article or blog post you'd like to read. Give yourself a good fifteen to twenty minutes to savor and enjoy it.

Today Jot down the article or blog post you're going to read. Make it a positive, uplifting piece.

_____

_____

_____

_____

_____

_____

_____

_____

_____

_____

_____

_____

_____

A New Take Time to reach back into the tool kit! Reframe a difficult or traumatic situation by retelling the story using humor. Make it the most hilarious story ever told. Embellish, add silly details, and laugh like you mean it. You are not dismissing the pain of what has occurred. You are, however, creating a new imprint in your memory to defuse some of the pain.

Today Rewrite your old story as if it were the funniest thing that has ever happened. Laugh out loud. Share it with someone you trust and invite them to laugh along with you.

_____

_____

_____

_____

_____

_____

_____

_____

_____

_____

Emotional Resilience Trait #8 Resilient people, HeartMath found, know who to go to for balanced, rational advice. If you are facing a dilemma, try to determine who in your circle will be able to give honest feedback and who will just add drama. Adding drama to a complicated situation will be nothing more than a distraction. Those whom can provide objective feedback or opinions serve to help you see other options at your fingertips.

Today Write about at least one person in your life who can give you honest feedback and not disrupt your process by trying to tell you what to do.

_____

_____

_____

_____

_____

_____

_____

_____

_____

Listening Can you hear me? Actively listening and reflecting back to another person what they've just said boosts their self-esteem. It's a lovely, gentle form of flattery, and shows that you genuinely want to understand their way of thinking and feeling.

Today Who is one person you want to listen to more actively in the next 24 to 48 hours?

_____

_____

_____

_____

_____

_____

_____

_____

_____

_____

_____

_____

Bump Up Your Game Remove your mobile distraction: your smartphone. These inventions are amazing tools for efficiency and connection. But they can, at times, be a complete distraction in social situations.

Today Write about the next get-together, gathering, or workplace meeting you have coming up. How will you manage your device so that you are not distracted by it?

➤ **The best thing you can do is to just turn your phone off. FOMO (fear of missing out) means you're not being present with the people right in front of you.**

_____

_____

_____

_____

_____

_____

_____

_____

_____

Stop and Smell the Roses Simple pleasures are sometimes easy to identify and access. Consider savoring that cup of coffee or tea. Perhaps take in the sunshine or go where you can breathe clean air. Enjoy something as simple as the purr of a cat—anything that feels positive to you. When you're feeling anxious or negative, access that memory and focus on it. It is another way to reteach your brain and carve positive pathways.

Today Write about one or two simple pleasures you can relish. Mark them with your favorite highlighter pen so they jump off the page as you thumb through your journal.

_____

_____

_____

_____

_____

_____

_____

_____

_____

Ancient Wisdom A 2008 integrative psychology study by
Matthew B. James for Walden University showed how the
ancient Hawaiian practice of forgiveness, *ho'oponopono*, reduces
the negative effects of guilt, shame, regret, and resentment associated with unforgiveness (i.e., the lack of forgiving someone).

In the 1970s, Hawaiian healer Morrnah Nalamaku Simeona distilled ho'oponopono into a simple, self-focused
application of the practice: a four-line mantra that can be
said anywhere, at any time, even to yourself, to bring inner
peace.

> *I am sorry.*
>
> *Please forgive me.*
>
> *I love you.*
>
> *Thank you.*

Today Slowly say the above ho'oponopono mantra, repeating
it three times. Pause. Write about your experience.

_____

_____

_____

_____

_____

_____

Tying It Together One of my favorite inspirational sayings about hope comes from the Bible, Hebrews 11:1: "Now faith is the substance of things hoped for, the evidence of things unseen." At times, you may not know what steps to take to reach your goal, the thing you hope for to improve your day, but faith in a higher power allows you to believe it is possible—even without any tangible proof that it could be.

Today Write about the hope, dream, or wish—which is ultimately a goal—requiring you to have faith.

➤ **Having faith is a very personal matter. With that said, so is your own interpretation of "higher power."**

_____

_____

_____

_____

_____

_____

_____

_____

Finding Clarity If and when it ever becomes too difficult for you to find your way to hope or even to know what the next steps may be, practice this simple technique: Ask your divine self to show you where to go and what to do next. Repeat the words *Show me.* It may take some time (days or longer) for you to see the next steps you will need to take. Be patient. Clarity will come.

Today Write about a time when you were locked into fear or inaction. How did you find your way out of the situation?

_____

_____

_____

_____

_____

_____

_____

_____

_____

_____

Music Therapy In a study by the US Department of Veteran Affairs, researchers found within a sampling of six thousand adults that 60 percent of men and 51 percent of women have experienced at least one traumatic incident in their lifetime. Music therapy was found to be a useful tool to reduce symptoms of those experiencing trauma, such as reducing the reliving of events and interrupting intrusive memories.

Today Consider the music that calms your mind, spirit, and soul. Create a playlist for yourself this week.

_____

_____

_____

_____

_____

_____

_____

_____

_____

_____

Seeing the Light "We cannot change what we are not aware of," Sheryl Sandberg has remarked. "And once we are aware, we cannot help but change."

Today Reflect on a recent moment of awareness you have experienced. Write about how it has improved your life.

_____

_____

_____

_____

_____

_____

_____

_____

_____

_____

_____

_____

Boost Self-Care According to a study published in the social psychology journal *Personality and Individual Differences*, there is a strong correlation between individuals who practice gratitude regularly and those who also engage in self-care behaviors such as exercise, eating healthy, and seeing their doctor.

Today Write about how your practice of gratitude is influencing your self-care routines.

_____

_____

_____

_____

_____

_____

_____

_____

_____

_____

_____

Recognizing Strength Throughout this process, you have written thank-you notes or e-mails to the people who have enriched your life. Now it's time to write one to yourself.

Today Write a thank-you note to yourself, acknowledging your strength and power. Remember these details for tomorrow's gratitude practice.

_____

_____

_____

_____

_____

_____

_____

_____

_____

_____

_____

_____

Twenty-Minute Rule A groundbreaking 1885 study by German psychologist Hermann Ebbinghaus identified the "forgetting curve": a formula that graphs the strength of one's memory, the length of time passed since first learning new information, and how these factors are beneficially impacted by spaced repetition, or repeated review of the original material after set amounts of time. Without repetition, we retain only about 58 percent of new material learned or memorized after twenty minutes. Let's focus on the routine of gratitude.

Today Reflect on how often you feel or express gratitude. Has it become a habit for you? Write about why or why not.

➤ **We will continue to form a practice of gratitude through repetition so that it becomes an unconscious habit supporting your resilience.**

_____

_____

_____

_____

_____

_____

_____

Dig Deep Summing up the last reserves of your inner strength and confidence in the nick of time is called "digging deep." Runner and entrepreneur Maggie F. Keenan explains it as the moment your legs feel like they're about to give out, just before you reach the finish line. Digging deep means finding the kick to finish the race when all your known energy seems to be depleted.

Today Write about your version of digging deep. What is it and how does it feel when you move beyond what you thought were your limits?

_____

_____

_____

_____

_____

_____

_____

_____

_____

New Perspective on Goals As we read in Week 29/Day 6, Dr. Chan Hellman and Casey Gwinn contend that hope is what leads you in the direction of achieving a goal. Hope is the motivator of that goal.

Today Write about a current goal you may have. Reflect and ask yourself if you truly have hope that it will be obtained.

_____

_____

_____

_____

_____

_____

_____

_____

_____

_____

_____

_____

_____

_____

Being Completely Honest What goal would you like to set that you've never shared with anyone else? Being honest with yourself is important. So is knowing what your fears may be.

Today Identify that goal and the fears that you have about venturing forward.

➤ Next month, we're going to go a little deeper into your more formal goals. So take the time now to really think about what you want.

_____

_____

_____

_____

_____

_____

_____

_____

_____

_____

_____

When in Doubt In Week 31/Day 1 we discussed placing tasks on autopilot. According to financial executive Robert Pozen, the most productive people "routinize" tasks that they consider low-priority—picking out clothes for work, choosing what to eat for lunch—to conserve energy for situations that are more important.

Today Think about which tasks in your daily routine are low priority and write about a few you could put on autopilot.

_____

_____

_____

_____

_____

_____

_____

_____

_____

_____

_____

_____

Self-Care Teeter-Totter You want to exercise, but the day gets away from you. Meditation seems to work wonders for others, but you just don't have the time. Part of this avoidance comes down to decision fatigue. However, if you plan your week out and schedule in gym time with a buddy or commit to taking a class, the decision has already been made in advance. You will go.

Today Sketch out your weekly schedule. Which days will you commit to a self-care activity? Block that time out in your calendar. If you would like a partner to go with you, send them a text once you've mapped out the schedule.

_____

_____

_____

_____

_____

_____

_____

_____

_____

Refilm It Neurolinguistic programming practitioner Matthew Walters asks his clients to tell him the story of a particularly uncomfortable or traumatic event. Then he asks them to retell the story as if it were the funniest thing that ever happened to them. For example, while creating this journal, my father passed away from Alzheimer's. Ever the escape artist, as a former cop, Dad could always get out of a tough spot. At his wake, we told a hilarious version of his many escapes from facilities and hospitals over the years and how we'd need to seatbelt his ashes into the car and seal his internment box closed with superglue because "Stan will always try to elude us." We reframed the event for our family through humor, creating a new, more pleasant connection in our minds.

Today Rewrite a traumatic story with humor. Better yet, take that story to a friend and retell it. Their only job will be to listen and promise to laugh, and laugh a lot, along with you.

_____

_____

_____

_____

_____

_____

Flashback A specific photo, video, or scent can immediately transport you to connect with a memory or feeling that gives you joy.

Today Write about one of these elements and why it brings you to a place of happiness.

_____

_____

_____

_____

_____

_____

_____

_____

_____

_____

_____

_____

_____

_____

Listen to Your Inner Compass In her book *The Beautiful No,* author and producer Sheri Salata exquisitely illustrates this concept: "I believe we all have an inner compass, a directive that lives quietly behind the scenes and really is the mastermind behind most of our life decisions. This compass is a kind of patterned inclination—do we generally lean in the direction of the good stuff, or do we give our compass some attention and rechart our course only when we've made a mess of things?"

Today Write about where your inner compass is leading you.

_____

_____

_____

_____

_____

_____

_____

_____

_____

_____

_____

Raspberries, Please! In studies by the University of Washington, researchers found eating anti-inflammatory foods helps you become more resilient because it reduces the physical symptoms caused by stress.

Today Write about how your last few meals made you feel and how you can plan on eating more anti-inflammatory foods, such as berries, tomatoes, olive oil, leafy greens, and nuts.

_____

_____

_____

_____

_____

_____

_____

_____

_____

_____

_____

Discreet Grins Go a Long Way A subtle grin and laugh shared with a friend—or even with yourself—helps to improve mental performance by increasing blood flow to the brain and boosting mental acuity. Just the change in facial muscles while grinning triggers a positive emotional signal in the brain. It's like enjoying a pleasant secret with yourself or with others.

Today Write about the last time you exchanged a grin with someone. Think of something that was genuinely amusing. What was it? What was that feeling like?

_____

_____

_____

_____

_____

_____

_____

_____

_____

_____

Eustress Is Good Stress Yes, there really is *good* stress, even though it releases cortisol. Twentieth-century endocrinologist Hans Selye called it *eustress* (the prefix *eu-* means "well" or "good" in ancient Greek). He categorized eustress as the feeling of invigoration one gets by focusing on a challenging but tangible goal that is within close reach. As the Roman poet Horace wrote, it is a desire to "seize the day." Once the task is completed, cortisol levels return to normal.

Today Write about a time when you felt eustress in your life. What were you focused on achieving? Consider how you felt during the process and how your body reacted after the task was complete.

_____

_____

_____

_____

_____

_____

_____

_____

Rubber Bands and Willow Trees Resilient people are flexible but remain true to their feelings. They respond to challenges and crises with intermixed emotions—both negative *and* positive. For example, a 2003 study published in the *Journal of Personality and Social Psychology* tested the emotional responses of University of Michigan college students to the 9/11 terrorist attacks. Those who showed fewer symptoms of depression had responded to the events with positive emotions of gratitude and love while also feeling anger and fear. To blot out everything that is painful isn't healthy. But to receive it with some positivity builds emotional flexibility.

Today Consider your own emotional flexibility. Think about a stressful situation in your own life. Now, quickly write down the emotions you feel. Include both the negative and positive.

➤ Just an FYI, trauma is not always a direct experience. It can be experienced from a distance.

_____

_____

_____

_____

_____

_____

Make the Connection Turns out that kindness has a greater impact on you than it does on the person receiving it. Famed cellist and composer Pablo Casals once said, "I feel the capacity to care is the thing which gives life its deepest significance and meaning."

Today Write about how your kindness provides significance to your life.

_____

_____

_____

_____

_____

_____

_____

_____

_____

_____

_____

Taking Deliberate Action It's time to administer a deliberate act of kindness. Kindness means many things; it's a very personal activity. I hope you're finding this practice to be cathartic.

Today Write about two or three random acts of kindness you could perform today. With whom and why?

➤ **The reason why can be as simple as just because** *it will feel good.* **Or just because** *it is the right thing to do.*

_____

_____

_____

_____

_____

_____

_____

_____

_____

_____

_____

_____

_____

Equalizing the Event We often place too much emphasis on mistakes. As Michelle Obama said, "Failure is an important part of your growth and developing resilience. Don't be afraid to fail."

Today Write about what this piece of wisdom means to you.

_____

_____

_____

_____

_____

_____

_____

_____

_____

_____

_____

_____

Flip the Dialogue Does your inner critic often have a lot to say? Making a conscious decision to convert negativity into something positive trains your brain to find the good in *bad* things. First identify the negative feeling and then add the positive aspect. For example, when your inner critic tells you you're stupid because you made a mistake, flip it and say to yourself, "Well it wasn't comfortable, but I've learned to make the following adjustments next time." Then name those adjustments.

Today Divide the below space into two columns. On the left, make a list of five to ten things your inner critic is telling you. On the right, using the above process, write the positive flips.

_____

_____

_____

_____

_____

_____

_____

_____

_____

Emotional Resilience Trait #9 HeartMath says resilient people are self-reflective. In my work with leaders, this is a big attribute I ask them to consider. Can you be honest with yourself? Will you take time to reflect on your daily behavior and exchanges with others? But more importantly, will you use this information to change your approach?

Today Take a couple of minutes to reflect on your behaviors and interactions with others yesterday. What could you do better next time? What would you like to change?

_____

_____

_____

_____

_____

_____

_____

_____

_____

_____

Stepping-Stones Author Kendra Cherry offers that by taking baby steps when working toward a goal, you are less likely to become derailed or discouraged by what is still to be done along the way.

Today Write about the steps you have already taken toward a goal, and additional steps you can take in the future.

_____

_____

_____

_____

_____

_____

_____

_____

_____

_____

_____

_____

_____

Mirror Image Looking within is a helpful practice toward building resilience. It allows you the opportunity to revisit a situation or exchange and see where tweaks can be made during similar events in the future. Adjustments to one's behaviors or reactions are the bounce-back mechanisms of resilience. They help you learn that, despite any setbacks, you have the power to make changes for a better outcome next time.

Today Self-reflect on a recent situation or exchange. What changes can you make in your behavior to gain a more desirable result next time?

_____

_____

_____

_____

_____

_____

_____

_____

_____

_____

Triple Rs Psychotherapist and author of *The Power of Apology* Beverly Engel offers a clear-cut guideline to offering someone a meaningful apology: It should consist of a statement of regret for causing pain, an acceptance of responsibility for your actions, and a statement of willingness to remedy the situation. The same guideline applies when someone offers an apology to you.

Today Write about an apology you previously rejected from someone that you now realize you are willing to accept. What made the difference?

_____

_____

_____

_____

_____

_____

_____

_____

You May Never Get This Dr. Shawne Duperon, founder of Project Forgive, teaches about "the apology you'll never receive" as a means to overcome anger or resentment toward someone who has hurt you but, for whatever reason, is unable to verbalize an apology. It's the process of playing out the apology in your own mind. This will help you release your anger toward the individual, changing your disposition for the better.

Today Play out an apology in your mind or write it below. Then read it aloud to yourself. How does it shift your perception?

➤ It may take a couple passes to feel the release. Keep at it! Check out the video clip of this exercise on Dr. Duperon's website, www.projectforgive.com.

_____

_____

_____

_____

_____

_____

_____

_____

_____

Date_____   **Week 40 • Day 1**

Seeing Them When others are vulnerable with you, they show you a deeply personal side of themselves. It requires an enormous amount of trust for people to open up. What emotions does this evoke?

Today Write about the last time someone let you in. What was that experience like for you?

_____

_____

_____

_____

_____

_____

_____

_____

_____

_____

_____

_____

The Beat Down Psychologist Leon Seltzer says that to improve self-esteem, you need to stop judging yourself so harshly. When you stop beating yourself up, a more positive image of self emerges. Self-esteem and self-acceptance go hand in hand.

Today Write about what your life would look like if you stopped judging yourself.

_____

_____

_____

_____

_____

_____

_____

_____

_____

_____

_____

_____

Subtle Can Sneak Up on You In his book *Ambition: How We Manage Success and Failure Throughout Our Lives*, author and social psychologist Orville Gilbert Brim Jr. notes that "sometimes we don't know we are losing until the very end." If you are shocked by a setback, it's important to ask yourself why. There are usually subtle indicators along the way.

Today Write about the subtle indicators you may have missed in a current or previous setback.

_____

_____

_____

_____

_____

_____

_____

_____

_____

_____

Hitting the Pavement Hard It's important to stress that everyone experiences setbacks. Three-time mayor of New York City Michael Bloomberg was fired from the investment firm Salomon Brothers before he founded his highly successful business, Bloomberg L.P. Anna Wintour was fired from her fashion stylist job at *Harper's Bazaar* before becoming editor in chief of *Vogue*. Failures happen, and rebounding from them is always possible.

Today Write about a past or current rebound trajectory. How's it going?

_____

_____

_____

_____

_____

_____

_____

_____

_____

_____

Picky, Picky There are many things to be grateful for in life. At times, however, we become too picky because something or someone is not perfect. In the famous words of the title character in the film *Ferris Bueller's Day Off*, "Life moves pretty fast. If you don't stop and look around once in a while, you could miss it."

Today Write about three things in your life that you may have picked over and missed as an opportunity to express gratitude.

_____

_____

_____

_____

_____

_____

_____

_____

_____

_____

_____

Date_____   **Week 40 • Day 6**

Hidden Lessons Try looking back at your past to discover a lesson that may have come disguised as misfortune. What did you learn from the discomfort?

Today Write about that lesson and the gratitude you have for knowing better now.

_____

_____

_____

_____

_____

_____

_____

_____

_____

_____

_____

_____

_____

A Moment of Mindfulness Over the past thirty-nine weeks, you've logged your gratitude, acknowledgments, and accomplishments at the end of each month. Now we're going to ramp this practice up. Gratitude is the magic elixir both in healing from physical and emotional challenges and in building a resilient core.

Today Write about the one thing you feel you've accomplished in this practice. Just one.

_____

_____

_____

_____

_____

_____

_____

_____

_____

_____

_____

Therapeutic Options Touch therapies, suggests psychotherapist Mandy Kloppers, such as acupuncture, acupressure, massage, Reiki, and reflexology, are additional options with which you can try to experience the emotional and physical health benefits of human contact.

Today Write about the last touch therapy you may have experienced. Consider what your mood was like for the 24 to 48 hours afterward.

_____

_____

_____

_____

_____

_____

_____

_____

_____

_____

_____

Write It Out Ian Usher, coauthor of *7 Simple Steps to Goal Achieving Success*, suggests that goals should be written down not just once but as often as possible. Over time, we refine and adjust our desires.

Today Write about the top three to five goals you're working toward or would like to work toward.

_____

_____

_____

_____

_____

_____

_____

_____

_____

_____

_____

_____

_____

_____

The Desire to Learn Usher notes that setting deadlines for your goals is an effective way to keep focused.

Today Review the goals you wrote out yesterday. In a different color pen or pencil, write out the target dates for each of them.

_____

_____

_____

_____

_____

_____

_____

_____

_____

_____

_____

_____

_____

_____

Refining Your Headspace Embracing a mind-set of positivity and hope enables you to look at your goals optimistically.

Today Write about the level of positivity and hope you've built up over these past months.

➤ **You've been working on building up positivity through your journaling all along!**

_____

_____

_____

_____

_____

_____

_____

_____

_____

_____

_____

Filling In Each of us possesses a certain skill set. However, we may be missing a few that could help us achieve a specific goal or fulfill our dreams. Usher instructs us that it's important to identify what these skills are and how you will develop them or to take steps to get assistance from a knowledgeable person or resource.

Today Write about the skills you may be missing. Next to each, note how you will learn these necessary skills or who can help you fill that void.

➤ **We are all surrounded by brilliant people who can help us. Just look around. You don't have to do this by yourself.**

_____

_____

_____

_____

_____

_____

_____

_____

One Foot Forward Being in motion toward achieving your goal is paramount in exercising your self-confidence and hope for the future. Usher advises that no matter what your readiness may be, don't wait—move forward. One step at a time, every day.

Today Write out five to ten steps you can take toward realizing your goal. Even the tiniest steps count. Star the one you can take action on today.

_____

_____

_____

_____

_____

_____

_____

_____

_____

_____

_____

Carrying Through After a major health scare, my friend Suzanne committed to changing her lifestyle habits. It took months for her to find the hope, willingness, and strength to undertake the task. Like you, she created a list of baby steps that would help her get there. Each day, she checked one action off her list. At the end of ninety days, she felt accomplished and in charge of her health again. Repetition and baby steps, she says, helped her realize it was possible.

Today Write about the next right step for you to do that will help you carry through on achieving your aspirations, personally or professionally.

➤ Bookending your action steps within a 30-, 60-, or 90-day period helps make your commitment realistic—until it becomes a habit.

_____

_____

_____

_____

_____

_____

Celebrate! Reward yourself when you achieve a goal. You may have noticed that when you journal your gratitude entries, several times I've asked you to also log your accomplishments the next day. This practice is a small way to mark your progress and demonstrate your resilience. Resilient people are those who take action toward a better tomorrow. Achieving your goals reminds you of this.

Today Write about a mini or massive celebration you can plan for yourself upon completion of a specific goal you've set along this journey.

_____

_____

_____

_____

_____

_____

_____

_____

_____

_____

Finding Your Heart Michael's divorce came as a complete shock to him. He became disheartened when the realization that he would now be a part-time parent to his daughter hit him. As a way to cope with this loss, Michael decided to go back to school to become a teacher. He felt that if he couldn't be a full-time parent, he could help enrich the lives of other children by teaching them.

Today Consider the past few entries on goals and dreams. Would it help you set a goal to offset a loss, as Michael did? Or have you set a goal that has special meaning to you? Why is it meaningful?

_____

_____

_____

_____

_____

_____

_____

_____

_____

Another Possibility Exists Sheryl Sandberg and Dr. Adam Grant, coauthors of the best-selling book *Option B*, explain that previously, most people were thought to react in only two ways after experiencing a loss or traumatic event: They would break down (i.e., develop depression or PTSD) or they would bounce back. However, further research by psychologists shows a third possibility: *bouncing forward* and growing from the challenge.

Today Acknowledge how far you've come over the past several months. Because you have! What forward bounces have you made in your life?

_____

_____

_____

_____

_____

_____

_____

_____

_____

_____

_____

Redefining Meaning Dr. Grant explains that when people experience challenges, they're usually more motivated to help others, especially those who have gone through the same types of challenges. He states, "Helping people through the trauma that you've faced is not only something that gives your life meaning, it gives your suffering meaning."

Today Who could benefit from your experience?

_____

_____

_____

_____

_____

_____

_____

_____

_____

_____

Keeping It Positive Countless experts believe that starting your morning with something positive sets the tone for the entire day.

Today Write about the one simple, singular action you can take (or have already taken) to start your day on a positive note.

_____

_____

_____

_____

_____

_____

_____

_____

_____

_____

_____

_____

_____

Co-Destiny In *Option B*, Sandberg and Grant also advance the concept of "co-destiny," which was developed by a former thesis student of Grant's, a physician named Joe Kasper. Kasper defines co-destiny as a means of doing good in honor of someone you may have lost. It's a way to continue the good work of your loved one, as if they passed their baton to you. And it's really the best way to honor their life.

Today Write about a co-destiny action you've done in the past to honor a loved one.

_____

_____

_____

_____

_____

_____

_____

_____

_____

_____

Not Thinking About Yourself In a 2015 study at the Yale School of Medicine, researchers found that, in the span of a day, those who helped others with simple tasks like holding the elevator or opening doors more often had higher levels of positivity and lower levels of stress.

Today Write about the kindnesses you have distributed over the past few days. Remember, small gestures mean a lot.

_____

_____

_____

_____

_____

_____

_____

_____

_____

_____

_____

Purple Bands Reverend Will Bowen, founder of A Complaint Free World, believes our focus should be on making positive change in the world rather than griping about problems. In an effort to help his congregation in 2006, Bowen created the twenty-one-day Complaint Free challenge. Church members who accepted the challenge were given a purple bracelet and instructed to switch it from one wrist to the other every time they complained or griped. Those who kept the bracelet on the same wrist for the entire challenge received a "certificate of happiness." The initiative soon went global; to date, more than eleven million people have taken Bowen's challenge.

Today Write about your ability to complete the Complaint Free challenge. Could you do it?

➤ Bowen says it takes most people four to ten months to go completely complaint-free for three weeks.

_____

_____

_____

_____

_____

_____

_____

What You Want Think about yesterday's challenge. Reflect on your experiences over the past twenty-four hours. How many times have you caught yourself slipping into negativity or complaining? Ah, to be human!

Today Write about any negative pattern you've observed in the past twenty-four hours that distracted you from focusing on positivity.

_____

_____

_____

_____

_____

_____

_____

_____

_____

_____

_____

Emotional Resilience Trait #10 The final resilience trait listed by HeartMath, and one of the most important, is that resilient people practice gratitude on a daily basis. For the remainder of the journal, we will make this a weekly practice.

Today List three things you're grateful for in your town or city.

_____

_____

_____

_____

_____

_____

_____

_____

_____

_____

_____

_____

Using the T-Word Part of resilience is the process of transforming ourselves and our lives from what they were to what we now consciously choose. In *The Beautiful No*, Sheri Salata calls it living her "unlived life"; transforming ourselves to become free of judgment from what may have been—missed chances or wasted time—to now step into what is possible. Salata writes, "It's about hope. . . . It is the seed of the tiniest momentum that propels you beyond the ruts you are stuck in, the routines you have so dedicatedly constructed over decades."

Today Write about the ruts you are now choosing to leave behind. And, if you dare, write about the possibilities of the *unlived life* you are willing to embrace.

_____

_____

_____

_____

_____

_____

_____

_____

Flip the Fear When failure is viewed as a threat, it creates a fight- or-flight surge in your body, according to happiness expert Tchiki Davis. However, choosing to view it as a challenge changes your mind-set and your body's reaction. A challenge-focused mind-set allows you to reframe the situation as something you're capable of resolving, so you'll be less likely to fail. Doing so bypasses that visceral reaction of fear.

Today Write about a current fear of failure and turn it into a challenge mind-set statement. For example, *I'm afraid I'll fail at restarting my life after divorce* could be repositioned as *I am taking on this restart as a challenge. I'm going to focus on what makes me feel happy, fulfilled, and exhilarated.*

➤ This is another example of finding that glimmer of hope and focusing on what you want rather than what you fear.

_____

_____

_____

_____

_____

_____

_____

Processing Grief Remember, grief and loss can pertain to many aspects of life—not just death. Another way to "complete" or move through the stages of a loss is to release any lingering emotional resentments. Of course, this is easier to read about than to actually do. Take baby steps!

Today Write about any festering resentments that are a result of a recent loss. Continue the journey of completion.

_____

_____

_____

_____

_____

_____

_____

_____

_____

_____

_____

_____

Repeat Often Freelance writer Zoe Blarowski offers the below four-step process to practicing forgiveness on a daily basis.

1. Think about someone who upset you or caused you pain.

2. Reflect on the emotions these thoughts bring up for a few moments, but then bring awareness to the fact that whatever was said or done happened in the past. There's nothing you can do now to change the outcome.

3. Try your best to embrace what you learned from the situation and let go of the rest.

4. Commit to moving forward now, without carrying emotional baggage left over from a past event you cannot change.

Today Write about your experience with this practice.

_____

_____

_____

_____

_____

_____

Musical Emotions In his book *Musicophilia: Tales of Music and the Brain*, Dr. Oliver Sacks wrote, "We humans are a musical species no less than a linguistic one. . . . We integrate all of these and 'construct' music in our minds using many different parts of the brain. And to this largely unconscious structural appreciation of music is added an often intense and profound emotional reaction to music." Researchers have found that people can successfully use music as a way to be more focused on a task, improve and influence their moods, and reduce stress.

Today Consider the music you listen to that helps you when you dive deeply into a task or hobby. What about its qualities helps you focus? Also worth noting is what type of music increases your stress levels.

_____

_____

_____

_____

_____

_____

_____

_____

Share Strength Sharing your personal experiences, journey, and lessons, says Michael Angier, author of *101 Ways to Be
Your Best*, is a gift to those around you. Often, we discount the
value in sharing these experiences.

Today Write about a personal experience that you believe
could be helpful for a friend or family member to hear.

_____

_____

_____

_____

_____

_____

_____

_____

_____

_____

_____

What You Want Research professor of psychology Dr. Sherry Hamby believes that those who share with others are inspired to summon their inner strength to overcome any situation. There is a saying in Alcoholics Anonymous rooms: "You can't keep what you have unless you give it away." Sharing and supporting others on their journey helps the giver maintain and remember the challenges they've overcome, too.

Today Write about a person who provided you with strength and inspiration through their own stories of resilience.

_____

_____

_____

_____

_____

_____

_____

_____

_____

_____

Pride Serotonin is released when we feel admired and recognized and when we feel proud of an accomplishment. While you may not necessarily define happiness and fulfillment with these feelings, we all possess the same neurochemical impulses.

Today Write about something you are particularly proud of or about a time when you felt deeply that others respected you.

_____

_____

_____

_____

_____

_____

_____

_____

_____

_____

_____

_____

Chocolate Chip Cookies The triggering of memories through sensory stimuli—specific flavors, smells, sounds, tactile feelings, and images—is referred to as the Proust Effect. Our olfactory sense in particular is a powerful memory tool. The smell of chocolate chip cookies baking may bring back pleasant memories from childhood, or the scent of a specific flower might remind you of a pleasant place.

Today Write about a specific scent or aroma that takes you back to a happy, safe place in your life.

_____

_____

_____

_____

_____

_____

_____

_____

_____

_____

Gratitude We can sometimes overlook the simple conveniences in our lives: running water, a car that works, a great neighborhood grocery store, or a helpful handyman. Noting and expressing gratitude for even the smallest good thing in our lives is important.

Today Make a list of five to ten everyday conveniences for which you are grateful.

_____

_____

_____

_____

_____

_____

_____

_____

_____

_____

_____

There's a Shot for That Researchers at King's College London found that we learn to cultivate an adaptive stress response to the negative effects of certain stressors—a form of immunity referred to as "stress inoculation." So the stress you feel now—depending on your threshold—may help you become more resilient in the face of a similar stressful event in the future. It is also theorized that early exposure to stressors seems to protect subjects from future hypersensitivity to stress.

Today Write about a stressor in your life that once caused you pain but that you are now able to glide past like it's nothing.

_____

_____

_____

_____

_____

_____

_____

_____

_____

Sweeping Out Clearing out old, musty, broken, or unneeded items is part of many people's seasonal house-cleaning ritual. It can also be a useful tool when it comes to relationships, work situations, or practices that leave you feeling stale, uninspired, or like you're participating only for duty's sake.

Today Write about one or two situations that you would like to sweep out so something new and fresh can come into your life.

➤ If you hear yourself saying, "Well, I have to do *X, Y,* and *Z,*" then you know it's a duty or obligation in your life. You may have just identified something to sweep.

_____

_____

_____

_____

_____

_____

_____

_____

_____

Willingness as a Catalyst HeartMath founder Doc Childre found that having an attitude of willingness is a catalyst for opening your life up to new opportunities and engagements. Willingness encourages curiosity, flexibility, humility, and receptivity. All are key ingredients to building resilience.

Today Write about your level of willingness to be open to newness in your life. Where are you *willing* to be flexible enough to look beyond what you are currently experiencing?

_____

_____

_____

_____

_____

_____

_____

_____

_____

_____

_____

Be Inspired Surrounding yourself with inspiration leads to living an uplifted life. Inspiration comes in many forms: painting, riding a bike, walking in nature, reading a book, and so on. The variations are as unique as you are.

Today What are five to ten things that provide you with inspiration and uplift you?

_____

_____

_____

_____

_____

_____

_____

_____

_____

_____

_____

_____

Overused but Important The rallying cry to be authentic can be a little annoying. However, the concept of really being yourself, Childre contends, is what's important. One key ingredient to reclaiming yourself is to be aware of your wants and desires. Then notice what comes up around what you *should* or *shouldn't do/say/feel* about these wants and desires.

Today Strip away the *should* and *shouldn't*. What desire or want have you buried away? Write about it and why you haven't acted on it.

_____

_____

_____

_____

_____

_____

_____

_____

_____

_____

Agile Brain Power According to ethologist Sergio Pellis, playfulness increases flexibility and adaptability. It also increases the ability to handle complex and unpredictable situations.

Today Write about an activity you do to help decompress from everyday challenges. It may be something that you've done since childhood.

_____

_____

_____

_____

_____

_____

_____

_____

_____

_____

_____

_____

Self-Directed Play Stuart Brown, author of *Play: How It Shapes the Brain, Opens the Imagination, and Invigorates the Soul*, encourages adults to engage in self-directed play. He contends that play makes us happier, smarter, and less stressed at any age. Play is a means of discovering, or rediscovering, who we are.

Today What's something fun and playful you can do during your day?

_____

_____

_____

_____

_____

_____

_____

_____

_____

_____

_____

Gratitude Loop Journaling gratitude on a regular basis creates more frequent feelings of gratitude. As we have seen throughout this journal, researchers have proven that gratitude triggers long-lasting and positive feedback loops. The more often gratitude is practiced, the longer you can maintain your positivity circuits.

Today Write about your experience over this past year regarding your gratitude practice on a regular basis.

_____

_____

_____

_____

_____

_____

_____

_____

_____

_____

_____

It Only Takes One Studies have shown that middle-aged adults who have at least one very close friend to turn to in times of crisis or upset have better overall health than those who do not.

Today Who is that person in your life? How does this friend support you?

_____

_____

_____

_____

_____

_____

_____

_____

_____

_____

_____

_____

_____

Three Criteria Relationships take time and effort. Psychologists Harry Mills and Mark Dombeck offer a simple framework to maintain relationships:

* *Know what your partner or friend expects from you.*

* *Try not to take them for granted.*

* *Make commitments and honor them with the necessary amount of time and effort.*

Today Consider the three criteria offered above. Which aspect(s) do you want to work on to strengthen an important relationship in your life?

_____

_____

_____

_____

_____

_____

_____

_____

Depth and Substance In a world of social media, where social currency is evaluated based on the number of friends, clicks, or likes you have, consider friendship in different terms: quality over quantity. Those who really care for you will be the ones willing to put themselves out there and help you. Invest your energy in those people.

Today Evaluate your current close relationships. Who are you willing to invest more time and energy into and why?

_____

_____

_____

_____

_____

_____

_____

_____

_____

_____

_____

_____

A Simple Guideline Author and motivational speaker Tony Gaskins offers simple, accessible guidance on boundaries: "You teach people how to treat you by what you allow, what you stop, and what you reinforce."

Today Based on how others treat you, what do you think you've taught them?

_____

_____

_____

_____

_____

_____

_____

_____

_____

_____

_____

_____

Live It Boundaries, according to researcher Amanda Furness, are the imaginary protective fields we place around ourselves to set limits on our time and resources. By setting healthy boundaries, we place ourselves in charge, choosing what and whom we allow into our lives.

Today Write about a healthy boundary you've set in your life that makes you feel protected and in charge.

_____

_____

_____

_____

_____

_____

_____

_____

_____

_____

_____

Date_____   **Week 46 • Day 6**

A Reminder A quote attributed to nineteenth-century French novelist George Sand reminds us: "Guard well within yourself that treasure, kindness. Know how to give without hesitation, how to lose without regret, how to acquire without meanness."

Today Write about these three aspects of kindness.

_____

_____

_____

_____

_____

_____

_____

_____

_____

_____

_____

_____

The Grass Is Just as Green An often-overlooked quality of people who are grateful is that they are less envious of others, less materialistic, and more likely to be generous with others, according to Russell Belk's materialism and dispositional envy scales, which measure the three sub-traits of materialism: envy, non-generosity, and possessiveness.

Today Write about an act of generosity you could extend to someone today.

➤ Every now and then, I'll anonymously pick up the tab for a stranger, just because. It makes my day and theirs, too.

_____

_____

_____

_____

_____

_____

_____

_____

_____

Truthfully, This Isn't Easy Being fully present with others, explains Dr. Emma Seppälä, isn't the easiest thing to achieve. Oftentimes you will feel frustrated because your mind will drift to another place while someone is speaking with you or you just can't focus on what's happening around you. Seppälä recommends establishing a meditation practice to center your mind. Books by Thich Nhat Hanh, Osho, or Pema Chödrön are good starting points.

Today Write about the apps you've looked at or research you've read on mindfulness and being present with others. List three or four, then asterisk the one you'll test out.

_____

_____

_____

_____

_____

_____

_____

_____

Speak Your Mind Make your voice heard, but do it politely. Addressing people you disagree with directly, and with civility and politeness, will go a long way toward resolving the issue. It will also bolster your understanding that you have control over your reactions.

Today Write about a past or present situation where you disagreed with someone. How could you politely address the issue with them?

_____

_____

_____

_____

_____

_____

_____

_____

_____

_____

_____

Finding Your Pathway Dr. George Bonanno defines resilience as the ability to maintain a stable equilibrium. He determined that there is no one path to building resilience. While there are common traits, each person creates their own balance.

Today Reflect on your journey through the ten traits of emotional resilience over the past year. You journaled about these traits on Week 7/Day 3, Week 11/ Day 3, Week 15/Day 3, Week 19/Day 3, Week 23/Day 3, Week 27/Day 3, Week 31/Day 3, Week 35/Day 3, Week 39/Day 3, and Week 43/Day 3. Write about the top three traits that you believe will help you find your stable equilibrium. There are no right or wrong answers.

_____

_____

_____

_____

_____

_____

_____

_____

_____

Date_____   **Week 47 • Day 4**

We Can All Do Better Even the occasional sleepless night can cause unnecessary moodiness. There are several lifestyle habits you can change to improve your sleep: reduce alcohol and nicotine consumption, engage in regular physical activity, remove distractions in your bedroom, utilize a quick five-minute meditation to relax, or explore behavioral techniques.

Today From the list above, which practice could you integrate into your daily ritual to help improve your sleep? Write about what that would be.

_____

_____

_____

_____

_____

_____

_____

_____

_____

_____

Supersurvivors The concept of "supersurvivors" was coined by psychology researchers and authors David Feldman and Lee Daniel Kravetz in their book *Supersurvivors: The Surprising Link Between Suffering and Success*. A supersurvivor is someone who transforms their life after experiencing a trauma and in spite of it, achieving amazing accomplishments in the process. That is bouncing forward. Everyone has a story that can inspire another person to not just bounce back but move forward and embrace hope.

Today Throughout this journey I have shared stories of my own and from others also on their resilience pathways. Reflect on your own journey. Write about one key element of your pathway that you can share with another person so they feel they can bounce forward, too.

_____

_____

_____

_____

_____

_____

_____

Self-Recognition According to Dr. Leon Seltzer, recognizing that you've done your very best in any given situation is a big part of healing negatively biased self-referencing beliefs. Those are the internal criticisms and judgments that play in the back of your head.

Today Write about a situation or quality of which you are self-critical. You may have an opportunity to re-spin the negative bias by recognizing that you've done your very best, even if you fell short.

_____

_____

_____

_____

_____

_____

_____

_____

_____

_____

Send Them Love Can't quite get to a place of forgiveness yet? Okay. Try this: Send the person who has hurt you *love*. It can be in the form of a smile or by treating them with kindness. If you're not able to see the individual (if they're not physically available or if it's too painful to address them face-to-face), visualization offers you the ability to extend love from afar.

Today Write about a situation that will require you to send someone love and kindness. What does that look like?

_____

_____

_____

_____

_____

_____

_____

_____

_____

_____

Dodgeball, Anyone? Living in a big city, it's sometimes hard to find good, old-fashioned, down-to-earth F-U-N. Recently a friend of mine stumbled across a game of kickball in Prospect Park, Brooklyn. Adults and children were playing and laughing together on red and blue teams. Enthusiastic onlookers were invited to participate in what was described as an utter blast, and the players were inspired to explore starting a kickball league. For days, my friend told and retold this story with much joy.

Today Write about an activity that inspires utter joy and laughter in your life. It could be something from your past—maybe kickball? Make a list of people you can engage with in this activity . . . soon.

_____

_____

_____

_____

_____

_____

_____

_____

To Be Clear Play theorist Brian Sutton-Smith offered this very clear distinction regarding the need for play in our lives: "The opposite of play . . . is not a present reality or work, it is vacillation, or worse, it is depression."

Today Write about how you can make your work or daily routine feel more playful.

_____

_____

_____

_____

_____

_____

_____

_____

_____

_____

_____

_____

Holding Hands Dr. Loretta Graziano Breuning determined that the release of oxytocin comes from feelings of trust and touch. Handholding can release small levels of oxytocin but over time builds a social level of trust between people.

Today Write about a person with whom you've felt this oxytocin release. Is there someone new, young or old, with whom you could hold hands? Or even just pinky lock? The release is the same.

_____

_____

_____

_____

_____

_____

_____

_____

_____

_____

The Gift of Uncertainty In *Habits of a Happy Brain*, Breuning writes that we often become frustrated by unwanted outcomes that result from choices we made in the face of uncertainty— or we dwell too much on roads not taken. Instead we should learn to honor our decision-making ability and to celebrate the uncertainty in our lives. Within uncertainty reside myriad options.

Today Write about an uncertainty that is evoking feelings of frustration. Would you, or could you, allow yourself to explore the possibility that there may be other options out there?

_____

_____

_____

_____

_____

_____

_____

_____

_____

Collecting Debts? Researchers at the University of Miami have found it's important to make a distinction between indebtedness and gratitude. Gratitude is felt in return for freely given acts of kindness, whereas indebtedness is felt if there is an understanding that you need to pay back someone for their kind act.

Today Write about an act of kindness you did that in actuality may have created a debt in disguise, or if someone did this to you. Occasionally we all make this error.

_____

_____

_____

_____

_____

_____

_____

_____

_____

_____

_____

Another Tidbit A study led by psychologist Martin Seligman found that participants who journaled three things they were grateful for on a daily basis for a week were 2 percent happier than before. Follow-up tests showed their happiness kept increasing: 5 percent after month one and 9 percent at month six. Why the increase? The participants continued the practice on their own.

Today Write about your plan to continue a practice of gratitude after this journaling period is concluded.

_____

_____

_____

_____

_____

_____

_____

_____

_____

_____

Powerful Catalyst Expressing appreciation to those who have been positive influences could sound like this: "Thank you for everything you've done to make me a stronger, wiser person."

Today Write a thank-you note to the individual who has inspired you to be just that—a stronger, wiser person.

_____

_____

_____

_____

_____

_____

_____

_____

_____

_____

_____

_____

_____

Intentional Distractions Neuropsychologist Rick Hanson emphasizes the enjoyment of life as a key component of resilience. Intentionally seeking moments of playfulness and enjoyment offsets stress and helps us connect more deeply with others.

Today Write about a few recent, enjoyable experiences that took you completely away from your everyday stress.

_____

_____

_____

_____

_____

_____

_____

_____

_____

_____

Daily Renewal In his volume of meditations titled *Buddha's Little Instruction Book*, Jack Kornfield wrote this inspiring reflection: "Every morning we are born again. What we do today is what matters most."

Today Write about your intention for the day.

_____

_____

_____

_____

_____

_____

_____

_____

_____

_____

_____

_____

_____

One More Note on Meditation In her book *The Happiness Track*, Dr. Seppälä encourages meditation as a means to cultivate a state of calm and decrease anxiety and fear about the future. Researchers have found that the minds of those who practice meditation have less tendency to wander.

Today Write about a meditation practice you may be able to integrate into your life. Remember that on Week 32/Day 3, we discussed coloring as a form of meditation. Be creative! What works for you?

_____

_____

_____

_____

_____

_____

_____

_____

_____

_____

Stuffing Down Emotions We regulate our emotions in many specific ways, found psychologist James Gross, director of Stanford's Psychophysiology Laboratory. One of the ways we regulate our emotions is by suppressing our inner feelings, but hiding them leads to adverse reactions, including having a worse memory for emotional interactions, higher blood pressure, and fewer close or positive relationships. Suppression also increases the negative impact of a traumatic experience.

Today Write about an experience you've had with suppressing emotions. What were the emotions you suppressed? And what further emotions were evoked—anger, fear, anxiety, dread?

_____

_____

_____

_____

_____

_____

_____

_____

_____

Four Reference Point Researchers at Ohio State University have established four principal points of resilience: autonomy (feeling that you have control over your life), camaraderie (having social support and a sense of community), opportunity (ways to accelerate your life), and meaning (being part of something important).

Today Write about one of these four points that you'd like to improve upon and why.

_____

_____

_____

_____

_____

_____

_____

_____

_____

_____

_____

Knowing What It Means Stress and burnout are different things and have different effects, say researchers at Ohio State. They define stress as being in a state of *overengagement*, where one has overreactive emotions and anxiety or hyperactivity. The main effect of burnout, meanwhile, is *disengagement*; the symptoms include withdrawal, emotional bluntness, depression, detachment, and sometimes feelings of hopelessness.

Today Were you feeling stressed or burnt out over the past few months? Write about the self-care practices and other resilience tools you used to rebound.

_____

_____

_____

_____

_____

_____

_____

_____

_____

Experiencing the Benefits Researchers have concluded that merely imagining being genuinely forgiven by someone whom you think you may have wronged can increase your feelings of gratitude and thankfulness.

Today Write about a person you may have wronged and how your imaginary apology makes you feel.

_____

_____

_____

_____

_____

_____

_____

_____

_____

_____

_____

_____

Insights Be willing to accept feedback and constructive criticism. Be gracious enough to offer the same to others. Author Liggy Webb calls this "the food of progress." Think of it as insights into learning how to tap your own personal potential as well as giving another the same gift. While it can be uncomfortable at times, it's important to become aware of your blind spots. Be discerning about what is offered to you. Not all feedback is accurate.

Today Pick one area of your life where you've resisted getting feedback. Write about moments when feedback from others has helped you gain valuable insights.

_____

_____

_____

_____

_____

_____

_____

_____

_____

Informing Your Boundary Setting boundaries doesn't necessarily tell people how to treat you, but boundaries do inform others as to what you will or will not tolerate. Remember: you can't control what other people do, but you can set a boundary around behavior directed toward you and control that.

Today Write about a time when someone may not have treated you kindly or respectfully. What boundary did you put in place in response to this? Did you learn how to enforce it?

_____

_____

_____

_____

_____

_____

_____

_____

_____

_____

_____

Reciprocity Respect the boundaries of others, even if you don't think they're necessary. Instead, find a way to behave so all parties feel comfortable. Be mindful not to build a barrier that feels like resistance rather than resilience.

Today Write about a boundary someone has set that feels incompatible for you. How will you discuss this with the person so resistance doesn't permeate your engagement with them?

_____

_____

_____

_____

_____

_____

_____

_____

_____

_____

_____

_____

Gratitude Attraction Researchers have found that people who are grateful increase their social capital with others and are considered to be nicer, more trustworthy, more social, and more appreciative.

Today Have you noticed any changes in your own social capital over the past year? How is this working for you?

_____

_____

_____

_____

_____

_____

_____

_____

_____

_____

_____

Pattern Principles As we have seen in previous prompts, studies show that people find meaning in mundane habits and patterns or routines. Assistant professor of psychology Samantha Heintzelman suggests that meaning can be found by maintaining a tidy office, grocery shopping, keeping a daily schedule, having regular dinners with friends, or driving the same route every day.

Today Write about the common threads in your daily activities and how they contribute to meaning in your life.

_____

_____

_____

_____

_____

_____

_____

_____

_____

_____

Developing a Mantra Sometimes we need a simple tool to help keep us on track. When you need to be reminded that every day is a random act of kindness, try using a mantra such as "I am able to extend kindness, compassion, and peace to _____."

Some suggestions to fill in that blank could be "my family," "my clients," "my colleagues," or "my neighbors."

Today Write the above statement ten times and fill in the blank with the same person or group.

_____

_____

_____

_____

_____

_____

_____

_____

_____

_____

Building Muscle Repetition builds muscle memory. Embracing a routine is a type of repetition.

Today Write about one routine you've embraced from this journal. What do you enjoy about it?

_____

_____

_____

_____

_____

_____

_____

_____

_____

_____

_____

_____

_____

_____

_____

Useful Resistance Mental health counselor Elena Yee discusses the concept of "radical acceptance" as a means to accept a difficult situation while also making changes—mindful acts of resistance—that feel more meaningful for your future. Resistance, in this context, is a constructive tool to positively, proactively build resilience while acknowledging reality and practicing acceptance.

Today Write about an example where you have accepted a given situation—despite not agreeing with it—and went quietly about your business making changes so the future would yield a different result.

_____

_____

_____

_____

_____

_____

_____

_____

_____

Boundaries Can Be Flexible Flexibility. There's that word again—and it's something to consider. As you grow, change, and have new experiences, Amanda Furness recommends being flexible with boundaries. There is an important distinction to be made between boundaries and barriers. Flexibility ensures they are not the latter.

Today Write about a time when you had to update one of your old boundaries. Why did you decide to do so? What was the end result?

_____

_____

_____

_____

_____

_____

_____

_____

_____

_____

A Big Boost Furness found that setting personal boundaries builds self-confidence and may bring more love, support, and respect into your life over time.

Today Write about the happy by-products of setting boundaries in your life. Are you more confident?

_____

_____

_____

_____

_____

_____

_____

_____

_____

_____

_____

Gratitude Moments Thinking back over the past few days, consider what moments of learning and insight you experienced. Each one is an opportunity for you to become a better person or professional. Take a moment to consider what a gift they may be.

Today Write a short list of five to ten teachable moments you're grateful to have experienced.

_____

_____

_____

_____

_____

_____

_____

_____

_____

_____

_____

Fabulous Failure Psychologist, coach, and writer Lisabeth Saunders Medlock offers us nine ways to move past fearing failure. We all make mistakes; when we do, the first lesson is to understand that those mistakes can help us determine what we really want in life. Mistakes focus our attention on what we need to fix in order to get back on the right path.

Toda Write about a mistake you made that gave you this type of clarity. Did you learn what you truly do and do not want?

_____

_____

_____

_____

_____

_____

_____

_____

_____

_____

_____

Who, Me? Dr. Medlock's second lesson about learning from our mistakes is that mistakes help us to accept and to love ourselves regardless of our flaws, warts, imperfections, and occasional shortcomings.

Today Write about a mistake that made you appreciate yourself more.

_____

_____

_____

_____

_____

_____

_____

_____

_____

_____

_____

_____

_____

Accepting Fallibility You may stumble, fall, and fail over and over again, but the experience is a powerful lesson, says Medlock. It teaches you to ask for assistance and enlist other people to help you get unstuck.

Today Write about a time when your tribe helped you get unstuck from a situation.

_____

_____

_____

_____

_____

_____

_____

_____

_____

_____

_____

_____

Honesty and Transparency No one likes to share that they've messed up or admit that they're truly afraid of being embarrassed. But acknowledging the truth, Medlock explains, helps us to know ourselves better.

Today Write about something you made transparent that taught you something about yourself you didn't know.

_____

_____

_____

_____

_____

_____

_____

_____

_____

_____

_____

_____

_____

_____

Analyze This Failures and mistakes teach us how to analyze problems and gain insight. Medlock suggests asking yourself, "How can I use this experience?" or "What will I do differently next time?"

Today Write answers to those questions based on your last perceived failure.

_____

_____

_____

_____

_____

_____

_____

_____

_____

_____

_____

_____

_____

_____

Adulting Medlock reminds us that failure teaches us to take responsibility for our choices. "Adulting" means that you've moved beyond blaming someone else and can accept outcomes as your own.

Today Write about a time when you witnessed another person take responsibility for their mistakes. What did it feel like to watch this act of bravery?

_____

_____

_____

_____

_____

_____

_____

_____

_____

_____

Integrity Breaking your promises, overcommitting and under-delivering, or failing to fully listen to others can be considered mistakes, Medlock notes. They may seem small, but they snowball over time. Having integrity means reexamining our motives and intentions when this happens.

Today Write about a time when you compromised your integrity. How did you remedy the situation?

_____

_____

_____

_____

_____

_____

_____

_____

_____

_____

_____

Engage or Retreat Mistakes, missteps, failures, or fumbles present a choice: Retreat, or fully engage in the world around you. When you engage, you are stretching yourself. Medlock suggests you do just that!

Today Write about a current stretch you're experiencing in your life. And please—applaud yourself for doing so!

_____

_____

_____

_____

_____

_____

_____

_____

_____

_____

_____

_____

_____

The Hidden Gift Medlock's ninth and last lesson is that sharing our failures and mistakes publicly can sometimes serve as an inspiration to others. Bouncing back, rebounding, and having resilience to persevere in the face of human error can be inspiring. Your experiences might help someone make an important change that they've been afraid to face.

Today Has someone you know inspired you through their fearless acts? Have you witnessed them admitting their errors or facing their fears?

_____

_____

_____

_____

_____

_____

_____

_____

_____

_____

Thank-You Notes Periodically, I've prompted you to write a thank-you note to someone to express your gratitude. Appreciation and validation are powerful tools to move people through building resilience. They are reminders that there is something good in every experience or exchange.

Today Write a thank-you note to yourself. Please thank yourself for your commitment to this process and all you have learned along the way.

_____

_____

_____

_____

_____

_____

_____

_____

_____

_____

_____

A FINAL PROMPT

A final piece of wisdom attributed to Marcus Aurelius:

"Dwell on the beauty of life.
Watch the stars, and see yourself running with them."

Today and for Always Go and do just that!

_____

_____

_____

_____

_____

_____

_____

_____

_____

_____

_____

_____

_____

_____

CONTRIBUTORS AND SOURCES

Teresa Amabile is the Baker Foundation Professor and Edsel Bryant Ford Professor of Business Administration, Emerita, at Harvard Business School. She is coauthor (with Steven Kramer) of *The Progress Principle: Using Small Wins to Ignite Joy, Engagement, and Creativity at Work*.

Michael E. Angier is the founder and president of SuccessNet.org and author of several books, including *101 Ways to Be Your Best*.

Roy F. Baumeister is a social psychologist and the Francis Eppes Eminent Scholar in psychology at Florida State Univ. He is coauthor (with John Tierney) of *Willpower: Rediscovering the Greatest Human Strength*.

Lee S. Berk is an associate professor of health promotion and education at Loma Linda Univ. He studies the effects of laughter on mental and physical health.

Zoe Blarowski is a freelance copywriter for health and medical companies.

Charlie Bloom is a psychotherapist and a relationship expert with a master's in social work.

Linda Bloom is a licensed clinical social worker, psychotherapist, and relationship expert.

George Bonanno is a professor of clinical psychology at Teachers College, Columbia Univ. He is considered a pioneer in the field of grief, trauma, and resilience.

Pauline Boss is an educator and a researcher recognized as the leading authority on the theory of ambiguous loss. She is the author of *Loss, Trauma, and Resilience: Therapeutic Work with Ambiguous Loss*.

Will Bowen is a minister, the founder of the A Complaint Free World organization, and author of five books, including *A Complaint Free World: How to Stop Complaining and Start Enjoying the Life You Always Wanted*.

Marshall Brain is the founder of HowStuffWorks.com, the director of the Engineering Entrepreneurs Program at North Carolina State Univ., and the author of numerous books.

Loretta Graziano Breuning is professor emerita of management at California State Univ., East Bay, and the author of eight books, including *Habits of a Happy Brain: Retrain Your Brain to Boost Your Serotonin, Dopamine, Oxytocin & Endorphin Levels*.

Orville Gilbert Brim Jr. was director of the MacArthur Foundation Research Network on Successful Midlife Development. His books include *Ambition: How We Manage Success and Failure Throughout Our Lives*.

Brené Brown is a research professor at the Univ. of Houston, a noted speaker, and the best-selling author of numerous books, including *Dare to Lead: Brave Work. Tough Conversations. Whole Hearts.*

Stuart Brown is the founder of the National Institute for Play and the author (with journalist Christopher Vaughan) of *Play: How It Shapes the Brain, Opens the Imagination, and Invigorates the Soul*.

Susan Cain is a cofounder of the Quiet Revolution and the author of two best-selling books, including *Quiet: The Power of Introverts in a World That Can't Stop Talking*.

Pablo Casals is considered one of the most gifted cellists in history. He was also a composer and a conductor.

Kendra Cherry is an educational consultant and the author of *The Everything Psychology Book*.

Doc Childre is the founder and chairman of the HeartMath Institute. He has written and contributed to multiple books, including *Transforming Stress: The HeartMath Solution for Relieving Worry, Fatigue, and Tension* (with Deborah Rozman).

James Clear is an entrepreneur, a photographer, and the author of the best-selling book *Atomic Habits: An Easy and Proven Way to Build Good Habits and Break Bad Ones.*

Amy Cuddy is a social psychologist, a Harvard Business School lecturer, and the best-selling author of *Presence: Bringing Your Boldest Self to Your Biggest Challenges.*

Dani DiPirro is a noted positivity blogger and the author of several books, including *The Positively Present Guide to Life: How to Make the Most of Every Moment.*

Mark Dombeck is a licensed behavioral psychologist who works with adults and couples to resolve painful life problems.

Shawne Duperon is a speaker and consultant on communication and engagement with an expertise in good gossip. She is the founder of Project Forgive.

Emeka Ekeke is a lecturer at the Univ. of Calabar in the Department of Religious and Cultural Studies.

Robert A. Emmons is one of the world's leading scientific experts on gratitude. He is a professor of psychology at UC, Davis, and the founding editor in chief of *The Journal of Positive Psychology.* He is the author of several books, including *Thanks!: How the New Science of Gratitude Can Make You Happier.*

Masaru Emoto was an entrepreneur who explored the possible effects of human consciousness on water and wrote numerous books, including *The Hidden Messages in Water* and *The Healing Power of Water.*

Beverly Engel is a psychotherapist and the author of more than twenty books, including *The Power of Apology: Healing Steps to Transform All of Your Relationships.*

Ubong Eyo is a lecturer at the Univ. of Calabar in the Department of Religious and Cultural Studies.

Lara Fielding is a clinical psychologist and the author of *Mastering Adulthood: Go Beyond Adulting to Become an Emotional Grown-Up.*

Barbara Fredrickson is the director of the Positive Emotions and Psychophysiology Laboratory at UNC, Chapel Hill. She is the author of *Positivity: Top-Notch Research Reveals the Upward Spiral That Will Change Your Life.*

Elliot Friedman is the William and Sally Berner Hanley Associate Professor of Gerontology in Human Development and Family Studies at Purdue Univ.

William F. Fry is the emeritus adjunct clinical associate professor in the Department of Psychiatry and Behavioral Sciences at Stanford Univ. He is also one of the founders of gelotology, the study of laughter.

Millard Fuller was the founder and former president of Habitat for Humanity International.

R. Buckminster Fuller was a twentieth-century architect, inventor, designer, and futurist known for his inventive and visionary approach to design and sustainability.

Amanda Furness is a research fellow in the Center for Genomic Medicine at Massachusetts General Hospital.

Tony Gaskins is a motivational speaker, a life coach, and the author of many books, including *Make It Work: 22 Time-Tested, Real-Life Lessons for Sustaining a Healthy, Happy Relationship.*

Pamela Palladino Gold is a speaker, inner-strength coach, and author of *Find More Strength: 5 Pillars to Unlock Unlimited Power and Happiness.*

Billi Gordon was a neuroscientist, writer, and actor.

John M. Gottman is a psychological relationship researcher, the founder of the Gottman Institute, and the best-selling author or coauthor of numerous books, including *The Science of Trust: Emotional Attunement for Couples.*

Adam Grant is a psychologist, a contributing *New York Times* op-ed writer, and the author or coauthor of several books, including the best-seller *Option B: Facing Adversity, Building Resilience, and Finding Joy* (with Sheryl Sandberg). He is the Saul P. Steinberg Professor of Management at the Wharton School of the Univ. of Pennsylvania.

Natalia Bailey Groat is a registered dietician at the Univ. of Washington's School of Public Health.

Casey Gwinn is the president and a cofounder of the Alliance for HOPE International.

Sherry Hamby is a research professor of psychology at Sewanee: The Univ. of the South. She is also the director of the Life Paths Research Center and the founder of ResilienceCon.

David R. Hamilton is an organic chemist, an inspirational speaker on kindness, and the author of ten books, including *The Little Book of Kindness: Connect with Others, Be Happier, Transform Your Life.*

Rick Hanson is a neuropsychologist at Duke Integrative Medicine and the author of *Resilient: How to Grow an Unshakable Core of Calm, Strength, and Happiness.*

Jennifer Read Hawthorne is a coauthor of four books in the Chicken Soup for the Soul series.

Samantha Heintzelman is an assistant professor in the Department of Psychology at Rutgers Univ.

Chan Hellman is a professor in the Anne and Henry Zarrow School of Social Work at the Univ. of Oklahoma and the founding director of the Hope Research Center.

Raymond Holliwell was a metaphysician and the author of several books, including *Working with the Law: 11 Truth Principles for Successful Living.*

Charles Hunt is a resilience expert, a motivational speaker, and the founder of the Audacity Firm.

Katie Hurley is a licensed clinical social worker and the author of three books, including *No More Mean Girls: The Secret to Raising Strong, Confident, and Compassionate Girls.*

John W. James is the founder of the Grief Recovery Method and a coauthor of several books, including *The Grief Recovery Method Handbook: The Action Program for Moving Beyond Death, Divorce, and Other Losses* (with Russell Friedman).

Matthew B. James, or "Dr. Matt James," is the president of the Empowerment Partnership and the author of several books, including *Ho'oponopono: Your Path to True Forgiveness.*

Robert Karen is a practicing clinical psychologist and psychoanalyst and the author of *Becoming Attached: First Relationships and How They Shape Our Capacity to Love.*

Maggie F. Keenan holds a doctorate in higher education from the Univ. of Georgia and is the founder of the Savannah, Georgia–based event Woman to Woman Connect.

Mandy Kloppers is a writer and a cognitive behavioral psychotherapist.

Steven Kramer is a developmental psychologist, independent researcher, writer, and consultant. He is a coauthor (with Teresa Amabile) of *The Progress Principle: Using Small Wins to Ignite Joy, Engagement, and Creativity at Work.*

Daniel J. Levitin is a cognitive psychologist and neuroscientist at McGill Univ., a musician, and a best-selling author whose books include *This Is Your Brain on Music: The Science of a Human Obsession.*

Matthew Lieberman is a professor and the director of the Social Cognitive Neuroscience Laboratory at UCLA.

Daniel Lumera is the founder and director of the My Life Design Foundation and the president of the International School of Forgiveness.

Fred Luskin is considered a leading authority on forgiveness. He is director of the Stanford Univ. Forgiveness Project and the author of several books, including *Forgive for Good: A Proven Prescription for Health and Happiness*.

Sonja Lyubomirsky is a professor of psychology at UC, Riverside, and the author of two books, including *The How of Happiness: A New Approach to Getting the Life You Want*.

Steve Maraboli is an author and a motivational speaker. His coaching program focuses on breaking habits and improving performance.

Rod Martin is a laughter researcher and a professor emeritus of clinical science and psychopathology at Western Univ. in London, Ontario.

Michael McCullough is a professor of psychology and the director of the Evolution and Human Behavior Laboratory at the Univ. of Miami. He is the author of *Beyond Revenge: The Evolution of the Forgiveness Instinct*.

Lisabeth Saunders Medlock is a clinical psychologist, consultant, coach, writer, and speaker.

Herman Melville was a nineteenth-century American novelist best known for writing the classic novel *Moby-Dick*.

Joshua Miles is an integrative psychotherapist.

Harry Mills is a consulting psychologist at AdventHealth Orlando in Florida.

Stephen Moeller is a licensed funeral director. He formed one of the first Grief Recovery Method support groups more than thirty years ago.

Carolyn Myss is a medical intuitive and the best-selling author of several books, including *Why People Don't Heal and How They Can*.

Amelia Nagoski is an associate professor of music at Western New England Univ. and a coauthor of *Burnout: The Secret to Resolving the Stress Cycle*.

Emily Nagoski is a sex educator and the best-selling author of *Come as You Are: The Surprising New Science That Will Transform Your Sex Life*. She is a coauthor of *Burnout: The Secret to Resolving the Stress Cycle*.

Kristin Neff is an associate professor of educational psychology at the Univ. of Texas at Austin and a pioneer researcher in the field of self-compassion. She is the author of *Self-Compassion: The Proven Power of Being Kind to Yourself*.

Sarah Kathleen Peck is a writer, a podcast host, a mastermind group coach, and the founder and executive director of Startup Pregnant.

Sergio Pellis is an ethologist at the Univ. of Lethbridge and the author of *The Playful Brain: Venturing to the Limits of Neuroscience*.

Lorna Phillips is a practicing attorney and the founder of Coaching for Conscious Leadership.

Robert Pozen is a senior lecturer at the MIT Sloan School of Management and a nonresident senior fellow at the Brookings Inst. He is also the author of several books, including *Extreme Productivity: Boost Your Results, Reduce Your Hours*.

Shekar Raman is a practicing neurologist.

Therese Rando is the clinical director at the Inst. for the Study and Treatment of Loss. She has also authored several books, including *How to Go on Living When Someone You Love Dies*.

Nancy Rothbard is the David Pottruck Professor of Management and the chair of the Management Department at the Wharton School of the Univ. of Pennsylvania.

Deborah Rozman is a behavioral psychologist, educator, and author, and the president and CEO of HeartMath.

Kelly Sullivan Ruta is a transformational coach, speaker, and former clinical social worker and psychotherapist.

Liz Ryan is a writer, a speaker, and the founder of the Human Workplace. She is also the author of *Reinvention Roadmap: Break the Rules to Get the Job You Want and the Career Your Deserve*.

Ralph Ryback is a psychiatrist with Sovereign Health Group, where he works on programs to treat addiction and mental health issues.

Sheri Salata is a writer/producer and a podcast cohost. She was formerly the executive producer of *The Oprah Winfrey Show* and served as a copresident of Harpo Studios and OWN, the Oprah Winfrey Network. She is the author of *The Beautiful No: And Other Tales of Trial, Transcendence, and Transformation*.

Sheryl Sandberg is the chief operating officer of Facebook and the founder of LeanIn. org. She is the best-selling author of *Lean In: Women, Work, and the Will to Lead* and a coauthor (with Adam Grant) of *Option B: Facing Adversity, Building Resilience, and Finding Joy*.

Martin Seligman is a pioneer in the field of positive psychology and the best-selling author of numerous books, including *Flourish: A Visionary New Understanding of Happiness and Well-Being*.

Leon Seltzer is a practicing psychologist, a writer, and the author of *Paradoxical Strategies in Psychotherapy: A Comprehensive Overview and Guidebook*.

János Hugo Bruno "Hans" Selye was a twentieth-century endocrinologist whose pioneering work in stress led to seventeen nominations for the Nobel Prize in Physiology or Medicine.

Emma Seppälä is the science director at Stanford Univ.'s Center for Compassion and Altruism Research and Education. She is the author of *The Happiness Track: How to Apply the Science of Happiness to Accelerate Your Success*.

Daniel J. "Dan" Siegel is a clinical professor of psychiatry at UCLA School of Medicine and a founding codirector of the Mindful Awareness Research Center. He is also the author of numerous books, including the best-seller *Mind: A Journey to the Heart of Being Human*.

Morrnah Nalamaku Simeona was a healer and practitioner of the Hawaiian practice of forgiveness, ho'oponopono.

Terry Small is a master teacher, speaker, leading learning skills specialist, and the creator and author of the *Brain Bulletin* newsletter.

Brian Sutton-Smith was one of the foremost play theorists and a prolific writer and author in the field.

Jill Bolte Taylor is a Harvard-trained neuroanatomist and the author of the best-selling memoir *My Stroke of Insight: A Brain Scientist's Personal Journey*.

Shelley E. Taylor is a distinguished research professor and the director of the UCLA Social Neuroscience Lab.

Jared Torre is a data scientist and researcher at Adobe and UCLA.

Neale Donald Walsch is the best-selling author of the Conversations with God series and many other books.

Matthew Walters is a hypnotherapist, soulmate coach, and cofounder of Creating Love on Purpose®.

Orna Walters is a soulmate coach and a cofounder of Creating Love on Purpose®.

Liggy Webb is an expert speaker and a consultant on resilience and behavioral agility and the founding director and CEO of the Learning Architect. She is the author of several books, including *Resilience: How to Cope When Everything Around You Keeps Changing*.

Steffanie Wilk is the associate dean for Diversity and Inclusion and a professor of management and human resources at Ohio State Univ.

Cathy Wong is a certified nutrition specialist and a wellness journalist.

Elena Yee is a mental health counselor at Marist College.

William P. ("Wm. Paul") Young is the best-selling author of the novels *The Shack*, *Cross Roads*, and *Eve*.